HERBS

A Guide to Growing, Cooking, and Decorating

Contributing Writer: Carol Landa Christensen
Consultant: Kathi Keville
Projects Coordinator: Don Newcomb

PUBLICATIONS INTERNATIONAL, LTD.

Contributing Writer: Carol Landa Christensen
Consultant: Kathi Keville
Projects Coordinator: Don Newcomb
Contributing Project Designer: Maria Buscemi
Illustrator: Roberta Simonds
Model: Pamela Kaplanes/Royal Model Management

Special thanks to Maureen Buehrli of The Herbal Connection and to David Merrill at *The Herb Companion* magazine.

Carol Landa Christensen has been a feature writer for the Springfield (Massachusetts) newspapers for the past nine years, and has contributed to various magazines, including *Plants Alive* and *Gurney's Gardening News.*

Kathi Keville is the author of *American Country Living: Herbs* and *An Illustrated Encyclopedia of Herbs,* and the editor of the *American Herb Association's Quarterly Newsletter.* She has also written approximately 100 articles on herbs for national magazines.

Don Newcomb is Chairman of the Horticulture Department at Triton College, where he teaches classes in floral design, manages their botanic garden and greenhouses, and sponsors frequent flower shows.

Photo credits:

Front cover: Sam Griffith Studios (top right & bottom right); **Tom Tracy Photography** (top left, center & bottom left).

Back cover: Tom Tracy Photography.

American Lamb Council: 35; **Walter Chandoha:** 54 (top right), 56 (top left), 58 (top left); **Steven Foster:** 52 (top left), 53, 54 (top left), 55 (top right), 56 (top right), 57 (top left & center), 58 (center), 59 (top left & top right), 60, 61, 62 (center & top right), 64; **Sam Griffith Studios:** Contents, 4, 7, 8, 9, 11, 12, 13, 15, 23, 24, 25, 27, 28, 29, 33, 42, 43, 44, 45, 46, 47; **International Olive Oil Council:** 32; **Kathi Keville:** 16, 56 (center), 63 (top left & top right); **Jerry Pavia:** 51 (top left), 54 (center), 57 (top right); **Joanne Pavia:** 51 (top right), 52 (top right), 55 (top left & center), 58 (top right), 59 (center), 62 (top left), 63 (center); **Photo/Nats:** 51 (center), 52 (center); **Tom Tracy Photography:** 26, 30, 34, 40, 49, 50.

Contents

Introduction

Herbs are probably the most popular and intriguing group of plants in existence. Undoubtedly, the explanation for this is that over the centuries herbs have been used in so many different ways. They flavor our foods, perfume our homes and bodies, decorate our gardens, and cure our ills.

Because of their diversity, no group of plants is more difficult to define. What exactly is an herb? There is no precise answer. Then how have we decided which plants to include in this book? We simply chose those herbs that we judge to be the most foolproof to grow and the most commonly useful—in cooking, potpourris, simple herbal cosmetics, and fresh and dried decorations—to a beginning enthusiast.

Sooner or later, most of us decide to try our hand at growing a few favorite herbs. Once started, many gardeners find themselves increasing the number of herbs they cultivate simply because so many of them flourish with very little care. These rugged hardy plants survive, and even thrive, in poor soil and wide temperature fluctuations that would prove too difficult for many other cultivated plant varieties. This same vigor makes them admirable choices for use in window boxes and other container situations where they're likely to be subjected to heat and dryness.

This book provides the basics on how to grow, propagate, harvest, and store the most popular herbs. It also includes ways on how to use them in your home and garden. Lists of herbs best suited for certain uses such as pot plants, potpourri ingredients, and fresh arrangements are handy for quick reference. The encyclopedia section features a photo of each herb along with notes on its culture, hardiness, harvest and storage techniques, and uses.

For culinary enthusiasts, there are lists of herbs whose flavors blend best with specific meats, vegetables, and beverages. Also included are some basic recipes for soups, sauces, stews, and marinades.

Herbs fit beautifully into any landscape. Ground-hugging thyme is a perfect choice for planting between the rocks in a flagstone walk. Tall clumps of angelica or rue provide attractive and dramatic accents in flower borders. Nasturtiums, calendulas, chives, and lavender all add outstanding floral color to a garden as well as attractive cut flowers.

Whether you want to grow a few herbs in your kitchen window as a source of fresh flavoring for your meals or you wish to design and plant an elaborate formal herb garden, the basic information you'll need to get started is provided here. As you become familiar with herbs, you'll probably find yourself gradually increasing both the amount and the varieties you grow, just as so many others before you have done!

Herbs are loved for their versatility.

Growing Your Own Herbs

Growing your own herbs assures a fresh supply each year. In addition, you know exactly what you're getting. There's no need for concern that any unwanted chemicals have been added — a matter of particular importance with culinary herbs.

Growing your own herbs can also provide other more aesthetic advantages. What can be more pleasant than the fragrance released by brushing past, stepping on, or rubbing between your fingers some foliage as you wander through your garden? Or would you prefer a foliar or floral focal point in a garden border, not to mention a unique addition to fresh or dried bouquets? Although you can certainly enjoy many of the pleasures afforded by herbs without growing them yourself, there is always an added measure of enjoyment when they're the product of your own effort.

This chapter will show you how to grow herbs from seed, cuttings, potted plants, division, and layering. It also provides information on basic requirements for good plant growth. Our chart quickly helps you identify those plants best suited to your site characteristics. It also notes whether plants are annuals (live one growing season), biennials (live two growing seasons), or perennials (may live up to 12 years), and how large you can expect each herb to grow when mature. Especially attractive landscape varieties are also identified. The soil and light section will even recommend ways to adjust your available conditions to better suit plants you may especially want to accommodate.

You'll discover that many herbs will succeed under a variety of growing conditions. You may even find yourself with more herbs than you can use. When you look at that tiny seedling or rooted cutting, it can be very difficult to believe that all you'll probably need to keep you fully supplied is one or two plants of thyme, sage, rosemary, basil, parsley, mint, chives, tarragon, oregano, and marjoram.

You'll probably need more plants if you cook large daily amounts of special ethnic foods that all use the same herbs, or if you're going to use large quantities of herbs for the herbal vinegar, oil, bath, or wreath projects mentioned in this book. You will also want more plants for special landscaping designs.

You can always add more if you find you've underestimated. If you have an oversupply, herbs, whether growing plants or herbal products, are always welcome gifts. Most people are intrigued by herbs and enthusiastic about giving them a try. Sharing your produce and knowledge with others is yet another enjoyable aspect of growing and preserving herbs.

Herbs are an attractive addition to any garden.

SOIL AND LIGHT

Soil, light, and water are the three essentials for plant growth. While some plants are very specific in their requirements, others are wonderfully versatile. They'll grow almost anywhere.

Fortunately, many of the most popular herbs fall into the latter category. The key to success with herbs is to select those that prefer the quality of soil and the amount of water and light you have available. For example, if you have an area of rich, moist soil with sun only part of the day, that's the ideal location for rue, sweet woodruff, peppermint, and spearmint. Many herbs such as sage, thyme, chamomile, and oregano survive in bright sun and dry, rocky, or sandy soil that is fairly low in nutrients. As a result, it's relatively easy to grow these herbs successfully in many parts of the country without the rich garden loam and high water availability that ornamental garden plants frequently require.

Of course, it's also possible to manipulate soil, water, and nutrients to accommodate a specific plant's preference. If you don't have the right conditions to support a particular herb, you don't have to do without. The best approach in most instances is to grow them in containers. Single plants can be grown in standard pots; several can be planted together in window boxes, half-barrels, or very large pots. Multiple plantings can be made up of one variety or a group of different varieties. Just be sure to combine those species that like the same soil, water, and light conditions in any one container.

If you want to provide special soil conditions for a large number of herbs, fill an entire planting bed with the desired soil mix after removing the existing soil to a depth of 8 to 10 inches and choose herbs that do not produce deep tap roots. Another alternative is to construct a raised bed of the same depth. This latter choice works well where better drainage is needed, or where more height will allow better plant visibility. Natural soil such as compost, lime, sand, or peat moss can also be added to the existing soil.

Here are three basic soil mix recipes that will work well for most plant needs. Keep in mind that these are not absolutely precise proportions. Unlike cooking recipes, they can be varied somewhat without dire results.

SANDY, WELL-DRAINED MIX:
   2 parts medium to coarse sand*
   1 part perlite
   1 part potting soil or garden loam

AVERAGE SOIL MIX:
   1 part potting soil or garden loam
   1 part moistened peat moss* or compost
   1 part sand* or perlite

RICH, MOIST MIX:

    1 part potting soil or garden loam
    1 part moistened peat moss* or compost

*NOTE: Do *not* use ocean beach sand because of the salt it contains. Get sand from a sand pit or builder's supply store. Also, peat moss is acid, so avoid large amounts when growing alkaline-loving plants.

Even though light conditions are more difficult to manipulate, they can be artificially adjusted to some extent. For example, if an area is too hot and sun-filled, consider ways in which some shade can be provided. A fence or an arbor could be a quick shade source as well as an attractive permanent garden feature. Even simpler would be a planting of annual or perennial vines on a wooden or wire support. For a long-term shade source, consider shade trees and hedges.

When the problem is one of not enough light, the solutions are either to remove some of the shade by thinning existing trees and shrubs or to regularly shuttle plants in and out of the shaded area. To do this successfully, potted plants need to spend at least half of their days in a sunny location. Therefore, they should be of a small enough size or set on wheels.

Another way to supply additional light, especially for herbs being grown indoors, is with the addition of artificial light. Lengthen the sunlight hours or strengthen the existing light by placing grow lamps over the plants.

This lovely Shakespeare Garden is bathed in herbs.

HERB CHART

NAME	PLANT	LANDSCAPE	LIGHT	SOIL	HEIGHT (IN INCHES)	SPREAD (IN INCHES)	CULTURE
Angelica	B	X	FS,PS	A,M	60-72	36	E
Anise	A		FS	A,D	18-24	4-8	E
Basil	A	X	FS	R,M	18	10	E
Borage	A,B	X	FS	P-A	24-30	18	E
Burnet	P		FS	A	18	12	E
Calendula	A	X	FS	A	12-24	12	E
Caraway	B		FS,PS	A,D	24	8	A
Catnip	P		FS,PS	A-S	18-24	15	E
Chamomile	P		FS	A-P,D	9-12	4-6	E
Chervil	A		PS	A,M	18	4-8	A-D
Chives	P	X	FS,PS	A-R,M	8-12	8	E
Coriander	A		FS	R	24-36	6	E
Costmary	P		FS,PS	R	30-36	24	E
Dill	A		FS	A-S,M	24-36	6	E
Fennel	P		FS	R	50-72	18-36	E
Garlic Chives	P		FS	A-P	18	8	E
Geraniums, Scented	P	X	FS	A-R	VARIES	VARIES	A
Horehound	P	X	FS	A-P	30	12	E
Horseradish	P		FS,PS	A	36-60	18-24	E
Hyssop	P	X	FS,PS	A	18	12	A
Lavender	P	X	FS	S,P	36-48	18-30	A
Lavender-Cotton	P	X	FS	S,P	12-18	18	E
Lemon Balm	P		FS,PS	A-S,M	48	18	E,R
Lovage	P	X	FS,PS	R,M	60	30	A
Marjoram	P,A		FS	R	8-12	12-18	E
Nasturtium	A	X	FS,PS	A-P,M	12-72	18	E
Oregano	P		FS	A-S	18	12	E
Parsley	B	X	FS,PS	R,M	12	8	E
Peppermint	P		FS,PS	R,M	24-30	12	E,R
Rosemary	P	X	FS	S	48-72	18-24	A
Rue	P	X	FS	P,S	24	18	A
Sage	P	X	FS	S	20	24	E
Savory, Summer	A		FS	R-A	18	8	E
Sorrel, French	P		FS,PS	R,M	18	10	E
Southernwood	P	X	FS	ANY	30	24	E
Spearmint	P		FS,PS	R,M	20	12	E,R
Sweet Woodruff	P	X	S	R,M	6-8	6-8	D
Tansy	P		FS,PS	A-P	40	12-18	E,R
Tarragon	P	X	FS,PS	S-R	24	24	A
Thyme	P	X	FS,PS	P-A	1-10	12-18	E,R
Wormwood	P	X	FS	ANY	30-48	15-20	A

PLANT: A=Annual   B=Biennial   P=Perennial
LIGHT: FS=Full Sun   PS=Partial Shade   S=Shade
SOIL: P=Poor   A=Average   R=Rich   S=Sandy   M=Moist   D=Dry
CULTURE: E=Easy to Grow   A=Average   D=Difficult   R=Rampant Grower/Keep Restricted

STARTING YOUR OWN PLANTS

Herbs are easy to grow.

There are five different ways in which new plants come into being. The simplest and least expensive source is from seeds. This is the best way to propagate most annuals and perennials. Among the herbs on our list, those easily grown from seed are basil, calendula, nasturtium, chervil, chamomile, summer savory, caraway, and dill.

A second easy and inexpensive source is by division. You physically pull apart the roots of a large perennial plant to create several smaller ones. Beginners should try to choose plants that have roots that sprout from the base and more than one stalk. Simply pull a root clump from the plant and repot it. Among the herbs in this book that readily divide are thyme, spearmint, peppermint, chives, lemon balm, and sweet woodruff.

A third, more expensive plant source is purchasing potted plants from a nursery or garden shop. When there are no budgetary limitations, this is the quickest and easiest way to obtain an established herb planting. Of course, it's the only solution when no other source is available. Unless you have a friend who will share, it may be necessary to initially purchase at least one plant of rosemary, oregano, lavender, and specialty varieties of thyme, such as lemon and silver thyme. The same is true of certain unique flavors of mint. Many scented geraniums, tarragon, and horseradish do not produce seeds at all and must be either purchased or divided. Most annuals such as basil, borage, calendula, chervil, and dill are grown from seed or purchased.

The fourth source of new plants is through the taking and rooting of cuttings from perennials. To execute this method, segments of plant stems that will generate their own roots when cut from the parent are inserted into a growing mixture. Of the herbs listed in this book, those best propagated by cuttings are rosemary, lavender, and tarragon.

A fifth method is layering. Most perennial herbs with sprawling stems will work. Bend the stem without removing it from the plant, so that it touches the ground. Mound dirt over the stem, press the soil down, and keep it watered. When a root has formed, cut the stem from the mother plant. It can then be replanted. Hyssop, lavender, oregano, and rosemary are all easily propagated by layering.

STARTING FROM SEED

Seeds can be handled in one of two ways. They can be planted directly in the garden bed or vegetable row once the soil begins to warm. Or they can be first started in containers indoors and then transplanted to their final growing sites.

Those herbs best seeded in their permanent locations from the beginning include anise, borage, dill, caraway, summer savory, angelica, chervil, and coriander. These varieties don't survive transplanting well, and they don't like to have their roots disturbed. Many other herbs, such as nasturtiums, basil, calendula, parsley, chives, chamomile, and lovage, grow so quickly and easily from seed that they can be planted in place.

Some gardeners, especially those in areas with long cold winters, like to get a head start on spring by starting these species indoors in late winter, then transplanting them into the garden as young plants. And if seed is the only way to obtain them, you'll definitely want to start the slower-growing and more difficult to germinate herbs—marjoram, lavender, rosemary, rue, and wormwood—in advance of the summer growing season. Most annuals will be up in one to two weeks. Perennials take two weeks or longer.

No matter how you start seeds, be sure to label them so you know what has been planted where. Young seedlings can be difficult to identify correctly. It's easy to lose track of what you have.

Seeding Directly in Garden

1. Once the soil is warm, cultivate and rake the bed to loosen and break up any existing lumps. Smooth the area.

2. Plant the seeds, three to a cluster, 3 to 6 inches apart in rows or sections. Plant at a depth recommended on the seed packet. Some seeds need to be on or near the surface, while others sprout better in the dark beneath a soil layer. After seeding, pat down the soil where each cluster was planted.

3. When seedlings sprout and grow their first true leaves, thin each cluster, leaving only the strongest plant. As plants grow and begin to crowd each other out, remove every other plant so that the remaining ones have plenty of space, light, and air circulation.

HERBS FROM SEED

Angelica	Calendula	Chives	Horehound	Lemon Balm	Rosemary	Sweet Woodruff
Anise	Caraway	Coriander	Horseradish	Lovage	Rue	Tansy
Basil	Catnip	Dill	Hyssop	Marjoram	Sage	Thyme
Borage	Chamomile	Fennel	Lavender	Nasturtium	Savory, Summer	Wormwood
Burnet	Chervil	Garlic Chives	Lavender-Cotton	Parsley	Sorrel, French	

HERBS GROWN FOR THEIR SEEDS

Angelica
Anise
Caraway
Coriander
Dill
Fennel
Lovage
Nasturtium (unripe)

Starting Seeds Ahead Indoors

1. Start seeds 6 to 12 weeks before the outdoor growing season begins. Use a sterile starting mix to avoid loss from "damping off."* Fill a shallow container that has holes in the bottom with the mix and smooth gently. Sprinkle the seeds, either in rows or by broadcasting, evenly over the surface of the mix about ¼-inch apart. If you are planting seeds in small individual pots, plant 2 to 3 seeds in each (keep only the strongest one once they sprout). Cover with more mix to the depth recommended on the seed packet.

* "Damping off" is a fungus infection that strikes very young seedlings, causing them to simply lie down and die. It is best avoided by making sure that both the soil and the containers in which seeds are planted in are sterile.

2. Place the entire container in an inch or so of water. Be careful to keep the water level below the rim of the container. Leave it in the water for a half hour or so, allowing enough time for the water to seep up through to the surface of the starting mix. Remove the container from the water tray and allow the excess to drip out. Place the container where it will get at least 8 to 10 hours of light a day. You may have to supplement natural light with artificial light from grow lamps. Find a spot where the soil will be kept warm or use a heater cable, since soil warmth is important.

4. Mulching plants when they're 1½ to 2 inches high will help maintain an even soil temperature and moisture level as well as discourage weed growth. Mulch may not be the best answer if you have a slug, snail, or earwig problem. They are attracted to mulch and baby plants.

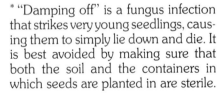

3. When the seedlings sprout, the first leaves to appear are what are known as the "seed leaves."

4. Transplant the tiny plants into regular growing soil in individual small pots or space them a couple of inches apart in plant boxes. Lift the young plants from underneath with a table knife or a spoon. Holding the plants by their base, gently separate them. Place the roots into a hole you've made with your finger or the knife. Plant the young plants at the same depth they were in the starter mix. Grow them in these pots or plant boxes until you are ready to plant them in permanent locations.

STARTING FROM CUTTINGS

Before taking cuttings, fill a container with a moist rooting medium—a mixture in which the cuttings will remain while they develop roots. Coarse sand used to be the standard rooting medium. Although it's still perfectly acceptable, there are now several other alternatives. One very good rooting medium is made by mixing perlite with an equal amount of either peat moss or vermiculite. Another is made by combining one part polymer soil additive (that has already been expanded with water) with two parts peat moss.

To take cuttings, use a sharp knife to cut 3- to 6-inch-long growth tips from the parent plant. Make a clean cut immediately below the point where a leaf attaches to the main stem. Avoid crushing the stem, which is essential for the cutting's survival while it has no roots. If you make a mistake, recut below another leaf higher up on the shoot. Carefully remove all leaves and leaf stems from the bottom one-half to two-thirds of the cutting.

Although use of a rooting hormone powder is not absolutely necessary, it does improve the success rate, especially for those herbs (such as lavender and rosemary) that are more difficult to root. Dip the lower third of the cutting into the powder, then gently tap the base of the cutting against the inside of the packet to shake off excess powder.

Ideally, no more than 15 to 20 minutes should elapse from the time that a cutting is removed from the parent plant to the time it's inserted into the rooting medium. If this is impossible, keep the cuttings in water during the interim and plant them as soon as possible.

With a knife blade or pencil, poke a hole in the moist rooting medium and insert the bottom two-thirds of the cutting into the hole. Use your fingers to firm the medium around the cutting stem. Insert additional cuttings into the medium with enough space between each so that the leaves just touch. Overcrowding will inhibit air circulation, which in turn will encourage the growth of undesirable fungi.

When all of the cuttings have been inserted, water the surface of the medium from above to further firm it around the cutting stems. Avoid getting water on the cutting leaves. Be sure to keep the soil damp continually while rooting the cuttings. Place the container where there is a generous amount of light, but no direct sun. Be sure to keep the rooting medium very moist. After a week to ten days, check to see if any roots have appeared. Insert a knife blade beneath one of the cuttings and gently lift it out of the medium. If there are no visible roots, carefully reinsert the cutting and firm the medium around it; check again in another seven to ten days. Some plants

take six or more weeks to root. Once the roots are ¼-inch long, plant them into a small pot.

Cover any large holes in the bottom of the pot with a piece of paper towel or small stones. Fill the pot with either a moist commercial potting mix or your own homemade mixture of moist soil. Check the encyclopedia section to see what kind of soil each herb prefers, then use the appropriate mix recipe found on pages 8 and 9. Poke a hole in the center of the soil with your fingers. Carefully lift the rooted cutting from the rooting medium in order to retain as many fragile roots and as much of the adhering medium as possible. Insert the rooted cutting into the hole. Firm the soil around the cutting and water the soil surface gently from above. Since excess water will drip out of the hole in the bottom of the pot, provide a drip tray. Don't allow plants to stand in water for more than an hour or two.

For at least a week or two, keep the potted cutting out of direct sunlight to avoid wilting. Grow it as a potted plant for at least a couple of months before tapping it out of the pot and planting it into a garden bed or a larger container.

The best time to take cuttings is during the mid-growing season, usually late spring or early summer, before the herbs have flowered.

Starting from Cuttings

1. Mix the rooting medium thoroughly and moisten it. Fill the container to within ¼-inch of the rim with the mixture. It should be at least 3 inches deep. Some good rooting mixes are one part perlite to one part peat moss *or* vermiculite, one part polymer soil additive to two parts peat moss, or clean coarse builder's sand.

2. Use a sharp knife to cut active growth tips from the parent plant. Cut just below the point where a leaf joins the main plant stem. The cut must be clean and smooth; if it isn't, try again below the next leaf up on the shoot. The finished cuttings should be 3 to 6 inches long. Dip the lower third of the stem into rooting powder.

3. With a knife or sharp fingernails, carefully remove all the leaves and leaf stems from the lower one-half to two-thirds of the cutting stem. Avoid leaving shreds or tears as these provide sites for rot, which will kill cuttings before they can root. If the remaining leaves are very large, trim off a few more lower ones to prevent excessive water loss through the leaves.

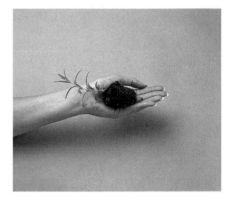

4. Poke a hole in the moist rooting medium with a knife blade or pencil. Insert the lower two-thirds of the cutting stem into the hole, making sure there are no leaves below the surface. Pack rooting medium firmly around the cutting stem. When all the cuttings are inserted, water from above to settle the medium further. Allow excess water to run out through the bottom holes.

5. Check the rooting progress every seven to ten days by gently lifting a cutting. When roots are ¼-inch long, plant them into regular potting soil in a small pot. Firm the soil around the stem and water from above after planting. Grow the cuttings in pots for at least a couple of months before moving them to a final site in the garden or to a larger container.

6. If the plants are in peat pots, simply dig a hole in the prepared garden bed and drop the plant, pot and all, into the hole. Peel off any peat rim that extends above the soil line. Water the plant in place. If plants are in pots, be sure the plant soil is moist. Hold the pots upside down with the plant stem between two fingers and knock the pot edge sharply against something solid. The soil ball will fall out into your hand, ready to plant. Plant at the same depth as in the pot. Firm the soil around the roots, form a soil dam in a circle around the plant stem, and fill the dam with water or mild fertilizer solution.

STARTING BY LAYERING

Another method of propagation is layering. This method is suitable for most perennials with strong stems. Herbs in the mint family are the easiest ones for the beginner to layer, although hyssop, oregano, rosemary, and lavender also work well.

Select an outer stem from the plant's base and gently push it down to the earth. Mound a pile of dirt on top of the stem, leaving at least five inches of the stem end uncovered. Pack the soil tightly and water the mound well. Continue keeping the soil well watered for the next several weeks.

Every few weeks, check for the appearance of roots. When they appear, make a quick, clean cut through the stem using a shovel or trowel to separate the layered herb from the original plant. Repot the new plant, being careful not to disturb the roots. Keep the new potted herb in a bright area away from direct light. In a couple of months, new leaves will start developing. Once they are well established, transplant the plant into a larger pot or into the garden.

Layering

1. Select an outer stem from the base of a plant that has strong, but flexible stems. Gently push the stem down to the ground.

2. Mound a pile of garden soil on top of the stem, leaving at least five inches at the end of the stem uncovered. Pack the soil tightly and water well.

3. Place a small rock over the mound of soil to keep the stem from springing back to an upright position. Keep the soil well watered for the next several weeks.

4. When roots appear, take a sharp shovel or trowel and make a quick, clean cut through the stem to separate the layered herb from the "mother" plant.

5. Lift the new little plant out of the ground and repot it. Be careful to disturb the roots as little as possible. Place the potted herb in a protected area in semi-shade or filtered light until it develops a sturdy root system.

Herbs In Containers and In the Garden

Although herbs are often planted in a very formal layout separate from the rest of the garden, this is by no means a requirement for success in growing them. Herbs can be mixed into other plantings. The exception is those few herbs such as mint, which will aggressively take over if not curbed. These are best planted in containers or separate beds, where their spread can be maintained.

Herbs can be laid out in a very formal or an extremely informal design or anywhere in between. The choice is entirely up to your personal view regarding what will fit best.

When planning a garden that includes herbs, the same basic rules of good design can apply as when designing any other garden. Tall plants can be located at the rear of side beds, plants of intermediate height in the middle of the bed, and low-growing plants at the front. This way they'll all be visible and will obtain a maximum share of the available light. In central beds that are viewed from all sides, the tallest plants can be located in the center of the bed, the shortest plants around the outer edge, and the intermediate heights between the two.

Because so many herbs have inconspicuous flowers, the beauty of their foliage and its color and texture become important design factors. Herbs with silver-gray, blue-gray, or purple foliage become dramatic accents among the greens.

Those with fine, fernlike leaves add a soft, airy look.

Even though all of these traits should be taken into consideration in your garden design, don't feel intimidated or overwhelmed by these details. Go ahead and lay out a plan to the best of your ability; then implement the plan without worrying that it must be "perfect."

After all, adjustments can always be made in the future. Unlike the building of a house, it's simple to change the details of a garden. Plants can usually be lifted and moved to a new location without harm.

The best approach to laying out a garden is to start by making a list of favorite plants that you'd like to grow. Then write down their soil, light, and water needs; their height and spread; and any special notes—such as foliage type or color, flower color, or unusual growth habit. Make a secondary list of those plants that you might enjoy having if there's any room left.

Sketch the garden area to scale (that is, 1 inch on the sketch equals 1 foot on the ground, or some other suitable proportion), decide on the size and shape of the planting beds, and determine which of the plants on your list will be located where in the beds. Once all of the varieties on your favorites' list have been used, fill in any empty spots with appropriate species from your secondary list.

Some Classic Formal Herb Garden Designs

Classic designs are typical of the formal balanced geometric layouts favored by wealthy Europeans of past centuries. They usually revolve around some sort of special garden feature, such as a fountain, sundial, garden seat, statue, an unusual feature plant, or birdbath. All paths and attention lead to this feature, whether it's in the center of the garden or along one edge.

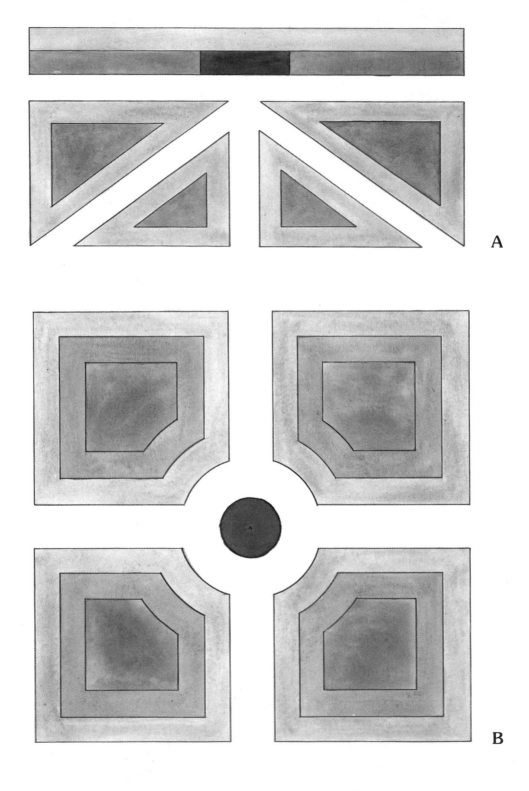

A

B

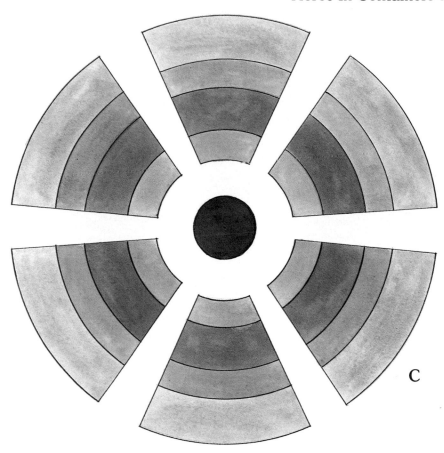

C

Monument

Wall/Fence

Low-growing

Medium-growing

Tall-growing

GROUP ONE – LOW

Dwarf Basil
Chamomile, Roman
Chives
Geraniums, Scented
Lavender, Munstead (trimmed)
Lavender-Cotton (trimmed)
Marjoram
Parsley
Rosemary, Creeping (trimmed)
Sweet Woodruff
Thyme

GROUP THREE – TALL

Angelica
Costmary
Fennel
Horseradish
Lavender
Lemon Balm
Lovage
Rosemary
Southernwood
Tansy
Wormwood

GROUP TWO – MEDIUM

Anise
Basil
Borage
Burnet
Calendula
Caraway
Catnip
Chervil

Coriander
Dill
Garlic Chives
Geraniums, Scented
Horehound
Hyssop
Lavender-Cotton
Nasturtium

Oregano
Peppermint
Rue
Sage
Savory, Summer
Sorrel, French
Spearmint
Tarragon

Some Informal Herb Garden Layouts

Here are two informal layouts. One stands as an island in the middle of a lawn area, and the other backs a wall or fence.

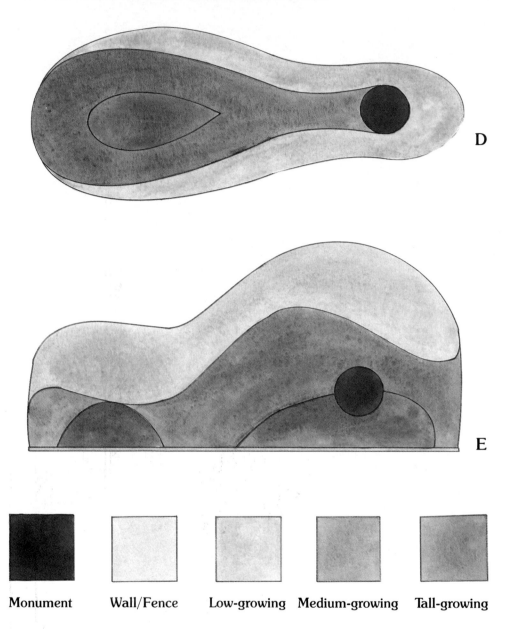

D

E

Monument   **Wall/Fence**   **Low-growing**   **Medium-growing**   **Tall-growing**

Layouts A, B, C, D, and E are planned so that you can use them in a do-it-yourself manner. Simply mark those herbs you like best in each of the three lists on page 19, then plug them into the spaces in the designs that match their group number. For example, if your favorites in Group One are thyme and chives, plant them in each space that is marked Low-growing on the plan you're following, etc.

You will easily see every plant if you carefully follow Garden Designs B, C, and D.

By choosing herbs of your choice from each group, Garden Designs A and E can look this enticing.

INVASIVE HERBS

Catnip	Oregano
Chamomile	Peppermint*
Chives	Southernwood*
Costmary*	Spearmint*
Garlic Chives	Tansy*
Horseradish*	Thyme
Lemon Balm	

*Worst offenders that require containment; others can be more easily kept in bounds by frequent removal of excess growth.

HERBS BEST SUITED TO CONTAINER GROWING

Basil	Parsley
Calendula	Peppermint
Catnip	Rosemary
Chives	Rue
Geraniums, Scented	Sage
Lavender	Savory, Summer
Lavender-Cotton	Sorrel, French
Marjoram	Spearmint
Oregano	Thyme
	Wormwood

HERBS BEST SUITED TO SHAPING

Basil
Geraniums, Scented
Lavender
Lavender-Cotton
Rosemary
Thyme
Wormwood

Harvesting, Preservation, and Storing

As a general rule of thumb, herbs have the highest level of flavor in their leaves just before they come into bloom. Therefore, harvests are best taken at this time. In the encyclopedia section you'll find notes regarding the best time to harvest each herb listed as well as the best methods of preservation.

You'll note that some herbs don't retain as much flavor when preserved by any means—they can only be used fresh. You can, however, extend their season by growing them indoors as pot plants during the winter months.

The most common method of herb preservation is by hang-drying. A method that is often used for drying more fragile herbs such as calendula petals and chamomile blossoms is by spreading them in a thin layer on a piece of clean wire screening. Another good modern way to preserve many culinary herbs is by freezing them. It's very quick and easy, and the flavor is usually closer to fresh than dried. If you have the freezer space available, freezing is probably the most desirable choice for cooking herbs.

Some herbs lose flavor when exposed to air, but they will retain it if stored in oil or liquor. Another way to capture herbal flavors is by extracting the essential oils from the plant leaves and stems through distillation. This latter method is not easily done at home, but it's possible to purchase these essential oils from specialty suppliers and health food stores when you want them.

The steps to follow for the drying, freezing, and storage of herbs are provided in this chapter along with step-by-step illustrations. In every case, the most important point is to pick the herbs at their peak, process them, and properly store them as quickly as possible. This way you'll obtain the best possible quality of herbal product. Delays will inevitably result in loss of essential flavors and perfumes.

HARVESTING

When harvesting herbs to preserve for future use, wait until the plant is at its aromatic peak. Pick it early in the morning when aromatics are at their highest level of the day. Discard any diseased or insect-infested portions. If there is dust present, wash the plant.

Be careful when harvesting seeds. The timing must be precise to allow the seeds to ripen completely, but they must be caught before they disperse. One way to solve this problem is to keep watch on a daily basis and to pick as soon as the seeds begin to dry. Carefully snip off the heads over a large paper bag, allowing them to fall into it. Let them remain in the bag to dry.

If you cannot keep such close track of the maturation process, another alternative is to enclose each seed head while still on the plant in a small paper bag once all flowering has ended and the green seeds become obvious. Then, when the heads dry, any seeds that fall out will be captured in the bag. Once you notice that seeds are being released, snip off the heads, bag and all, and dry them indoors.

Once harvested, follow the step-by-step instructions given on the next pages.

Homemade herbal oils and vinegars are a real treat.

DRYING

To dry fresh herbs, as well as fresh flowers that you might use in arrangements, first gather fresh branches of perennials or the entire annual plant in the early morning. Wash them thoroughly with plain water only if there is dust on them, since washing increases the loss of aromatics. Shake off as much water as possible; if the foliage is especially dense, pat it dry with towels.

The best location for drying herbs is in a dark place that is well ventilated, hot, and dry. An attic, barn, or shed loft; breezeway; or covered porch are good choices. Under these conditions, moisture will be quickly evaporated from the plant materials while most of the important aromatic oils remain.

Depending on the weather conditions, especially humidity, leaf and stem thickness, and other such variables, it will take anywhere from a day to a week to naturally air-dry various herbs. Check every day to see how the drying is progressing.

As soon as the leaves are fully dry, but before they become brittle, strip them from the stems and store them in airtight containers to preserve as much flavor and aroma as possible.

Air-drying herbs is easy.

Drying

1. Method 1: Group herb and flower branches into small bunches for rapid drying with good air circulation to avoid the possibility of mold growth. The size of the bunch depends on your local humidity. Bind the stems together with an elastic band and hang them upside down in a hot, dry location with little or no light.

2. Method 2: Remove petals from flowers and leaves from stems, spreading them thinly on a tray made of clean screening. Leave space between the pieces for air movement. Place the screen tray out of the wind, but where air can reach it from both the bottom and top in a hot, dry location with little or no light.

3. Method 3: Spread separate petals and leaves on a layer of paper towels. Place them in a microwave oven. Set on low for just one minute at a time; check often for degree of dryness. Remove them from the oven before they are fully dry and allow them to air-dry to avoid the possibility of overdrying.

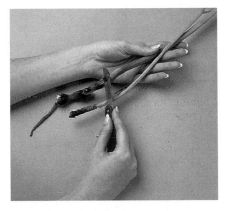

4. Method 4 (for seeds): Hang-dry bundles of plants as in Method 1, but place each bundle inside of a large brown paper bag that will catch the seeds. Alternatively, hang the bunches from poles laid across the open top of a large cardboard box that is lined with a sheet of paper.

5. Method 5 (for roots): Thoroughly scrub roots and split very thick ones lengthwise. Slice them into ¼-inch-thick pieces. Air-dry as in Method 2 or spread them on cookie sheets to dry in a regular oven at the lowest setting. Do *not* use a regular oven to dry any other herbs, as it will be too hot and they'll lose their aromatics.

HERBS EASILY AIR-DRIED (¼ to ⅓ of dried = fresh quantity)

Angelica	Chamomile	Hyssop	Oregano	Savory, Summer	Thyme
Anise	Coriander	Lavender	Parsley	Southernwood	Wormwood
Basil	Costmary	Lavender-Cotton	Peppermint	Spearmint	
Borage	Dill	Lemon Balm	Rosemary	Sweet Woodruff	
Caraway	Fennel	Lovage	Rue	Tansy	
Catnip	Horehound	Marjoram	Sage	Tarragon	

FREEZING AND OTHER METHODS OF PRESERVATION

The preliminary steps in preparing herbs for freezing are identical to those for drying. First gather fresh stalks and branches early in the morning when they have the highest concentration of aromatic oils. Wash them thoroughly in cool water to remove all dust, if necessary. Remember that washing increases the loss of aromatics. Shake off as much water as possible; pat dry with towels if foliage is especially dense.

For bouquet garni, break herbs into small sprigs; for addition to soups, stews, and other recipes, snip them into pieces with scissors or chop them with a knife or in a food processor. Mint or scented geranium leaves can be frozen whole, then removed and floated unthawed in punches and other cold drinks. Most frozen leaves don't make good garnishes because they become limp as they defrost. Use candied leaves and flowers instead.

Other Specialty Notes:
Peel, then chop or grate horseradish root to a fine paste, and loosely pack it in small jars; stir in a mix of 1 teaspoon salt dissolved in 1 cup of white vinegar. Be sure to stir out any air pockets. The herbs should be totally submerged. Prepare fresh ginger root the same way; combine and cover it with whiskey. Mix and cover peeled whole garlic cloves with vegetable oil.

Making bouquet garni.

Freezing and Other Methods of Preservation

1. Method 1: Separate herbs into small shoots or separate leaves; chop them as desired with a knife or scissors. Pack them in screw-top jars or sealable plastic bags, with as little air as possible, and immediately put them in the freezer for storage.

2. Method 2: Place the herb pieces in a blender or food processor with an equal amount of water. Chop them to desired size, pour them into ice cube trays, and freeze. You can also freeze whole leaves or flowers in ice cubes. When solid, transfer the cubes to storage containers and immediately return them to the freezer.

3. Candying: Pick and air-dry the stems, leaves, and flowers to be candied on paper towels. In a saucepan, add 1 cup sugar to ½ cup water. Cook on low heat, stirring, until clear. Partly cool and stir in 4 teaspoonfuls of gum arabic. Chill. Dip each item into the chilled mix, using your finger to spread it over the entire surface. Place the pieces on a cake rack to dry, turning them once after 12 hours. When totally dry, store them in tightly covered containers.

4. Salting: In a stoneware crock, alternate a ½-inch layer of fresh, chopped herbs and a ½-inch layer of non-iodized salt. Pound the herbs with a wood mallet or jar to eliminate air spaces. Both the herbs and the salt can be used for seasoning any time after the first month. (Also see page 33 for making herb vinegars and oils and page 34 for pesto and bouquet garni recipes.)

HERBS TO FREEZE

Angelica	Costmary	Nasturtium	Savory, Summer
Anise	Dill	Oregano	Sorrel, French
Basil	Fennel	Parsley	Spearmint
Chervil	Garlic Chives	Peppermint	Tarragon
Chives	Lovage	Rosemary	Thyme
Coriander	Marjoram	Sage	

HERBS TO CANDY

Angelica stems	Catnip leaves	Lavender flowers
Anise seed extract	Horehound leaves,	Peppermint leaves
Borage flowers	fresh or dried	Spearmint leaves

STORING HERBS

Careful storage of herbs is just as important as careful preparation and preservation. If any of these procedures is neglected, the end result will be loss of the essential oils—the source of an herb's flavor and perfume. Once the herbs are fully dry, there should be no delay in getting them stored in airtight containers with as little air space inside as possible. Also, ground or powdered herbs do not store as well as chopped herbs.

Containers suitable for storage of dried herbs are glass jars with tight-sealing lids or glass stoppers; tin canisters that can be tightly closed; plastic pill holders with tight covers; and sealable plastic bags, buckets, or barrels for large pieces. Frozen herbs should be stored in any available tightly sealed plastic, glass, or metal container.

Store them in a dark place in order to best preserve good color and flavor. If herbs must be stored in a lighted location, they should be kept in metal tins or dark-colored jars that will block out most or all of the light. Last but not least, clearly label each container with its contents and the date of harvest. Once frozen, it may become difficult to differentiate one herb from another, and after several seasons of harvest, it's impossible to remember what year different herbs were preserved.

A good practice is to discard any remaining supply of an herb as soon as a new supply is available. By promptly rotating out the surplus each season, you'll have high-quality, full-strength herbs on hand at all times.

Storing Herbs

1. As soon as they are dry but before they crumble when touched, remove the leaves, flowers, or seeds into a bowl. Leave them whole or crush them into a powder with a mortar and pestle.

2. Using a clean sheet of paper rolled into a funnel, pour the prepared herbs into containers.

3. Clean and dry the bowl, mortar, and pestle before processing the next variety. Label the container clearly with the name of the herb along with the year of harvest. Without labels it quickly becomes difficult to keep inventories straight.

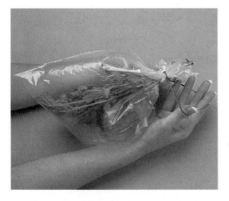

4. Store herbs in a dark place to preserve colors and flavors. If no such space is available, store them in tins with tight covers or in sealable jars made from dark-colored glass. Rotate out any surplus left from the previous season as soon as the new supply is available.

5. To store large pieces of herbs suitable for use in herbal baths and herb wreaths, lay thoroughly dried branches in large plastic bags. Seal the open end tightly with an elastic band. Store in a dark place or inside a cardboard box. Large pieces can also be stored in large plastic buckets or fiberboard barrels with tight-fitting lids.

Herbs can be stored in a variety of containers.

Cooking With Herbs

Nothing more effectively transforms a food from bland to delicious than the addition of one or more herbs. To prove this to yourself, simply mix a few chopped chives, dill, garlic chives, or caraway seeds into cream cheese or cottage cheese and use as a cracker spread.

Sprinkle a dash of salt, oregano, and tarragon along with a splash of white vinegar over canned chick-peas; kidney, green, or wax beans; canned asparagus; or any steamed or boiled vegetable leftovers. Serve cold as a tasty side dish. Adjust the proportions to your own taste, remembering that a little goes a very long way when using these strong aromatic ingredients. Substitute sage and marjoram for the oregano and tarragon and see how the flavor changes. Experiment with other combinations to discover which ones you and your family like best.

Once you've had some success adding herbs to a few foods, you'll become increasingly open to the idea of using them to vary your menu. Herbs can completely change the flavors of homemade soups, stews, vegetables, and breads. Even if you purchase rather than raise your own culinary herbs, the cost of this improvement will only amount to pennies a day.

Several basic recipes are included here. We hope you'll use them as a foundation on which to build. There are no hard and fast rules of combination or proportion; the ones provided here are those that have a fairly universal appeal.

If you study the ethnic favorites of any nationality, you'll discover that the ingredient lists differ primarily in the kinds and amounts of herbs and spices that are added, rather than in the kinds of meats and vegetables used. For example, Spain, France, Italy, Yugoslavia, and Greece have similar climates and foods available, and they cook these foods in similar ways. Obviously there is much overlap, and there are other important ingredient differences such as the kinds of olives, tomatoes, cooking oils, wines, cheeses, and hot and sweet peppers used. The flavors, nonetheless, are frequently very different. The Greeks add sage and licorice-flavored anise to their dishes, the Italians often use basil and oregano, the French prefer tarragon and rosemary, the Yugoslavs add paprika and poppy seeds, and the Spaniards favor bay leaves and saffron.

Our chart lists those herbs most frequently recommended to complement a number of basic foodstuffs: different meats, vegetables, beverages, baked goods, and fruits. Each time you prepare one of these foods, add a different one of the herbs listed and see what you think of the result. Note down the amount and kind of herb you used, and whether or not you liked it. Over time, you'll learn which herbs you enjoy most and the proportions you prefer.

Few kitchen utensils are needed to add herbs to food.

HERBAL OILS AND VINEGARS

Herb-flavored vinegars and oils are easy to make. Always start with a wine vinegar that has a pleasing flavor, since the original taste cannot be improved by the addition of herbs.

For an attractive appearance, select jars and bottles that have nice colors or shapes. It's a great way to recycle pretty glass bottles. Thoroughly clean and then sterilize recycled containers by steaming or boiling for 15 minutes. If food odors persist, discard the container.

You can identify each herb flavor by inserting a sprig of fresh herb into the bottle before filling it with the herbal vinegar. You can also use labels or tie color-coded yarn around the bottle necks.

Since herbal oils have a higher concentration of flavor than vinegars, they're added to recipes in much smaller amounts. Therefore, for the best flavor store herb oils in small containers and keep them tightly sealed at all times.

High quality olive oil is best, but any flavorless cooking or salad oil can be used. As with vinegars, a strong flavored oil will overpower subtle herb flavors.

Many herbs make good oil and vinegar choices.

Herbal Oils

1. Chop fresh, clean herbs and pack them loosely in a clean glass container, about one-third to one-half full. Fill the jar with room temperature oil. Cap the container and place it in a warm location. Stir or shake daily for three to five days.

2. Remove herbs by pouring them through a cheesecloth or a fine sieve. Test for flavor. Repeat the process with a new batch of fresh herbs if the flavor of the oil is too mild.

3. Pour the finished product into small bottles and jars with tight-sealing caps. Label and date.

Best herb oil choices: rosemary, dill, thyme, fennel, tarragon, garlic chives, savory, basil, coriander, marjoram, mint.

Vinegars

1. Pour vinegar over fresh, clean, chopped herbs loosely packed in a large glass (*never metal*) container. Use all of one variety or mix herbs, whichever you prefer. Fill the jar about one-third to one-half full with herbs and add vinegar to the top. Cap the container securely with an acid-resistant lid. Keep it at room temperature. Stir or shake well once each day for two weeks. An alternative method is to use whole herbs, which is attractive, although the resulting vinegar will be mild-tasting.

2. Taste a sample for flavor. Pour the vinegar through cheesecloth to strain out the herbs. Add plain vinegar to dilute it if the taste is too strong.

3. For decoration and identification, you can insert a sprig of fresh herb into each sterilized storage bottle, but this is optional. Pour herbal vinegar into a bottle and cap tightly. Cork stoppers can be sealed by dipping the jar top into melted paraffin wax once the stopper is securely in place. Label and date the vinegar.

Best vinegar choices: basil, dill, tarragon, thyme, chive blossoms, garlic chives, savory, marjoram, rosemary.

Basic Recipes

BOUQUET GARNI

For use in sauces or soup stocks, bouquet garni can be sprinkled directly into a pot or, for clear stock, enclosed in a clean cloth bag and removed from the liquid at the end of cooking time.

Recipe 1
Using Fresh or Frozen Ingredients
        3 sprigs parsley or chervil
            or both
        ½ bay leaf
        2 sprigs thyme
        1 stalk celery

Recipe 2
Using Dried Ingredients
        1 teaspoon dried parsley
        ⅛ teaspoon thyme
        ⅛ teaspoon marjoram
        ¼ bay leaf
        ¼ teaspoon celery seed

Variation
For winter squash or sweet potatoes: Equal parts angelica and bay leaves

PESTO

Pesto may be added to soups and stews as is. It may also be blended with milk, cream, or wine to make a sauce for pasta, fish, chicken, or fresh vegetables.

Basic Recipe
        1½ to 2 cups fresh or frozen
            herb leaves*
        2 large cloves garlic
        ½ cup freshly grated
            Parmesan cheese
        2 teaspoons freshly grated
            Romano cheese
        ½ cup olive oil
        ½ cup pine nuts or walnuts
        Salt and pepper to taste

Combine herbs, garlic, and cheeses in food processor. Turn on the processor and slowly add oil and nuts. Blend until a paste is formed. Season to taste. Pour into a glass container with a ¼-inch skim of plain oil on top and cover tightly. Store in refrigerator.

Variation
You can leave out the cheeses and garlic and freeze the pesto in serving-size portions (spoon it into ice cube trays, freeze, remove promptly, and permanently store them in tightly sealed freezer containers). Add cheeses and garlic when ready to use.

*Use any *one* of the following quantities and combinations:
        Option 1: 2 cups basil
        Option 2: 1 cup basil and 1
            cup watercress
        Other Options: ½ cup oregano
            (savory, sage, tarragon, or
            thyme) and 1½ cups parsley

Pasta With Pesto

Heartland Lamb Stew

FINES HERBES

Fines herbes are used in egg and cheese dishes, soups, and sauces. Mince fresh or frozen herbs together; to retain full flavor, add them at the last minute before removing the dish from heat and serving.

Basic Ingredients: equal parts of parsley, chervil, and chives
Optional Additions: thyme, tarragon, savory, or basil

HEARTLAND LAMB STEW

Makes 6 servings

1 to 1½ pounds boneless lamb shoulder, cut into 1½-inch cubes
3 tablespoons vegetable oil
¼ cup all-purpose flour
1 tablespoon sugar
2 teaspoons salt
1 teaspoon pepper
1 can (14½ ounces) tomatoes
2 medium onions, cut into quarters
3 whole cloves
1 clove garlic, minced
1 small bay leaf
¼ teaspoon dried rosemary, crushed, or 2 teaspoons chopped fresh rosemary
2 cups water
6 medium potatoes, pared, cut into quarters
6 medium turnips, cut into quarters
3 medium carrots, cut into thick slices
1 package (10 ounces) frozen cut green beans

Brown lamb in hot oil in ovenproof Dutch oven over medium-high heat. Drain drippings. Combine flour, sugar, salt, and pepper in small bowl. Sprinkle over lamb; stir to combine. Add tomatoes, onions, cloves, garlic, bay leaf, rosemary, and water. Cover and bake in preheated 350°F oven 30 minutes. Add potatoes, turnips, and carrots. Bake, covered, 30 minutes more. Adjust seasonings, if necessary. Add beans; bake, covered, 30 minutes more or until meat and vegetables are tender. Remove bay leaf before serving.

Favorite recipe from American Lamb Council, Inc.

35

FRESH TOMATO PASTA ANDREW

Makes 2 main-dish or 4 appetizer servings

    1 pound fresh tomatoes, cut into wedges

    1 cup packed fresh basil leaves

    1 tablespoon *each* fresh oregano and parsley leaves

    2 cloves garlic

    2 tablespoons olive oil

    8 ounces Camenzola cheese *or* 6 ounces ripe Brie plus 2 ounces Stilton cheese, each cut into small pieces

    Salt and white pepper to taste

    4 ounces uncooked angel hair pasta, vermicelli, or other thin pasta, hot, cooked and drained

    Grated Parmesan cheese

Place tomatoes, basil, oregano, parsley, garlic, and oil in covered food processor or blender; pulse on and off until ingredients are coarsely chopped, but not puréed. Combine tomato mixture and Camenzola cheese in large bowl. Season to taste with salt and white pepper. Add pasta; toss gently until cheese melts. Serve with Parmesan cheese. Garnish as desired.

Favorite recipe from California Fresh Market Tomato Advisory Board

VEGETABLE AND HAM SOUP

Makes 6 to 8 servings

    2 tablespoons margarine or butter

    1 medium onion, coarsely chopped

    2 tablespoons chicken flavor instant bouillon

    1 tablespoon Pesto or one Bouquet Garni (see page 34)

    1 large potato, peeled and diced

    1 (16-ounce) package frozen mixed vegetables

    2½ cups (10 ounces) Armour® Ham cut into ½-inch cubes

    Salt and pepper to taste

Melt margarine in Dutch oven over medium heat. Add onion; sauté until tender. Add remaining ingredients and 5 cups water. Bring to boil over medium-high heat. Reduce heat to simmer. Cook, uncovered, for 30 minutes, or until potato is tender. Garnish with carrot curls and fresh chives, if desired.

Fresh Tomato Pasta Andrew

BEEF FAJITAS

Makes 4 to 6 servings

¼ cup lime juice
¼ cup tequila
2 tablespoons vegetable oil
2 cloves garlic, minced
1 fresh or canned jalapeño
    pepper, stemmed, seeded,
    and minced
1 teaspoon *each* chopped
    fresh parsley, cilantro, and
    chives
¼ teaspoon salt
¼ teaspoon ground black
    pepper
1½ pounds beef flank steak
2 cans (about 16 ounces each)
    refried beans
8 to 12 flour tortillas,
    8-inch diameter

Condiments
    2 avocados
    Lime juice
    Salsa
    Sour cream

To prepare marinade, combine lime juice, tequila, oil, garlic, jalapeño pepper, parsley, cilantro, chives, salt, and black pepper in small bowl. Trim any visible fat from meat; place in heavy, self-sealing plastic bag. Pour marinade over meat; seal bag. Refrigerate 8 hours or up to 2 days, turning bag occasionally to distribute marinade.

Preheat charcoal grill and grease grill rack. Place refried beans in large skillet and heat through; keep warm. Stack and wrap tortillas in foil; place tortillas on side of grill to heat. Remove meat from marinade; reserve marinade. Place meat on grill 4 to 6 inches above solid bed of coals (coals should be medium-glowing). Cook, basting frequently with reserved marinade, 4 minutes on each side for rare or until meat is brown on the outside but still pink when slashed in thickest part. To serve, cut meat across the grain into thin slices; place on warm platter. Peel, pit, and chop avoca-

dos; sprinkle with lime juice. Place tortillas, refried beans, avocados, salsa, and sour cream in separate serving dishes. Wrap the meat and condiments in tortilla and eat out of hand.

Variation
Shrimp or Chicken Fajitas: Follow directions for Fajitas but use 2 pounds raw medium shrimp, shelled and deveined, *or* 2 pounds chicken breasts, boned and skinned, in place of flank steak. Add 1 teaspoon chopped fresh tarragon to marinade. Marinate 2 to 3 hours. To cook, thread shrimp or chicken on skewers. Place on greased grill 4 to 6 inches above a solid bed of coals (coals should be low-glowing). Cook shrimp, turning and basting frequently with reserved marinade, 3 to 4 minutes on each side or until pink. Cook chicken, turning and basting frequently with reserved marinade, 3 to 4 minutes on each side or until meat is no longer pink when slashed in thickest part.

Beef Fajitas

CULINARY HERB CHART
NOTE: Use herb *leaves,* except where otherwise noted.

MEATS

BEEF:
Angelica
Caraway seeds
Coriander seeds
Horseradish roots
Marjoram
Oregano
Sage
Savory, Summer
Sorrel, French

VEAL:
Basil
Chervil
Chives

LAMB:
Basil
Dill
Hyssop
Peppermint
Rosemary
Sage
Sorrel, French
Spearmint

PORK:
Angelica stems
Caraway seeds
Dill
Marjoram
Oregano
Rosemary
Sage

POULTRY:
Basil
Borage flowers
Calendula petals
Chives
Coriander seeds
Dill
Hyssop
Lovage seeds
Marjoram
Oregano

Parsley
Rosemary
Sage
Tansy
Tarragon
Thyme

SEAFOOD

SHELLFISH:
Basil
Chives
Coriander
Costmary
Dill
Oregano
Thyme

FISH:
Anise seeds
Basil
Borage flowers
Caraway seeds
Chervil
Chives
Costmary
Dill
Fennel
Horseradish root
Marjoram
Parsley
Rosemary
Sage
Savory, Summer
Tansy
Tarragon
Thyme

VEGETABLES

TOMATOES:
Basil
Dill
Lovage seeds
Oregano
Rosemary
Sage
Savory, Summer
Tarragon

POTATOES:
Basil
Caraway seeds
Chives
Coriander
Dill
Fennel seeds
Horseradish root
Lovage seeds
Marjoram
Oregano
Parsley

SALADS:
Anise
Basil
Borage flowers
Burnet
Calendula petals
Caraway
Chervil
Chive leaves, flowers
Coriander root
Fennel
Garlic Chives
Geraniums, Scented, flowers
Horseradish root
Hyssop*
Lemon Balm
Lovage leaves, stems, seeds
Nasturtium leaves, flowers
Parsley
Rosemary*
Sage*
Savory, Summer*
Sorrel, French
Tarragon*
*Salad seasoning only

PICKLES:
Borage flowers
Coriander seeds
Dill leaves, seeds
Lovage seeds
Nasturtium buds, flowers,
   flower buds, leaves
Tarragon

CHEESE DISHES

COTTAGE CHEESE:
Anise
Caraway seeds
Chives
Dill
Marjoram
Oregano
Parsley
Savory, Summer
Thyme

CHEESE SPREAD:
Borage flowers
Burnet
Calendula petals
Caraway seeds
Chives
Coriander seeds
Dill leaves, seeds
Fennel seeds
Garlic Chives
Geraniums, Scented, flowers
Lovage seeds
Marjoram
Oregano
Rosemary
Sage
Thyme

EGG DISHES

Chervil
Chives
Costmary
Fennel
Marjoram
Oregano
Parsley
Rosemary
Tansy
Tarragon

SOUPS

Angelica
Anise seeds

Calendula petals
Caraway leaves, roots
Chervil
Chives
Garlic Chives
Hyssop
Lovage stems, leaves
Marjoram
Parsley
Rosemary
Sage
Savory, Summer
Sorrel, French
Thyme

STEWS

Angelica
Anise seeds
Basil
Caraway leaves, roots
Chervil
Coriander seeds
Dill
Lovage
Marjoram
Sage
Savory, Summer

STUFFING

Marjoram
Sage
Thyme

BAKED GOODS AND BREADS

Angelica root, seeds, and
  candied stems
Anise seeds
Caraway seeds
Coriander seeds
Fennel seeds
Geraniums, Scented
Rosemary
Sage
Tansy

BEVERAGES

WINE PUNCH:
Burnet
Calendula petals
Sweet Woodruff

FRUIT DRINKS:
Borage
Costmary
Lemon Balm
Peppermint
Spearmint

TEA:
Angelica roots, seeds
Anise seeds, leaves
Catnip
Chamomile flowers
Geraniums, Scented
Horehound
Hyssop
Peppermint
Sage
Spearmint

CANDY

Angelica stems
Borage flowers
Horehound
Lavender flowers
Peppermint
Spearmint

JELLY

Anise
Geraniums, Scented
Lavender
Lemon Balm
Parsley
Peppermint
Rosemary
Sage
Spearmint
Thyme

Decorating With Herbs

Sprigs of herbs, whether fresh or dried, will make an aromatic and attractive addition to any home decor. The simplest way to enjoy them indoors is to cut stems of one or more varieties, arrange them in a vase, pitcher, or bean pot filled with water, and place them wherever a live accent is desirable.

Another easy way to use fresh herbs is as a filler in fresh floral bouquets. Mint, curly parsley, basil, rosemary, sage, and southernwood are all good choices.

Many herb flowers are decorative. Calendulas have large daisylike blooms throughout the summer ranging from lemon-yellow to intense orange in color; borage produces brilliant blue, star-shaped blossoms; tansy blooms are a strong-scented mass of small, bright-yellow buttons; and lavender provides abundant blue spikes early each summer. Nasturtiums give the most outstanding display of all. They bloom abundantly right up until frost in a tremendous range of brilliant colors.

Dried herbs can be used in a number of different decorative ways as well. The easiest is to simply tie several fresh branches tightly together and hang them upside down as sprays. They'll look great in the kitchen, dining room, or pantry.

A more formal look, appealing to use in any room in the house, can be achieved by making an herb wreath, heart, or crescent. Wood, wire, or plastic foam base forms for these pieces can be found at most craft stores and florist shops, or you can make your own. Simply attach the herbs by firmly wrapping them onto the form with florist wire or twine (those with stiff stems can simply be poked in if a plastic foam base is used).

Additional herbs, clusters of dried flowers, groups of whole spices such as nutmeg and cinnamon sticks, or decorative bows can be used to fill in any bare spots and to provide accents to the wreath once the foliage base is completed.

Mix foliages or make an entire wreath from a single variety. The fullness and impact of the wreaths will vary depending on the density and texture of the materials used. Bay leaf wreaths will look deep green, formal, sleek, and sculptured. Thyme produces a narrow, delicate, airy outline. Southernwood gives a heavy, dense, silvery result.

A way to enjoy herbal aromatics indoors is through potpourris and sachets. Potpourri can be used to lightly scent the air anywhere in the house. Sachets delicately perfume closed spaces such as linen and clothes closets, bureau drawers, and hope chests. For the most simple aromatic of all, toss a few fresh or dried sprigs into the fireplace or float them in a shallow pan of water heating on a wood stove or cooktop. It will instantly release a pleasing aroma to the entire house.

Herbs are such decorative plants!

MAKING AN HERB WREATH

Sooner or later, most herb gardeners find themselves with an excess supply of herbs. You don't need to discard anything. The best idea is to make an herbal wreath. They are very easy to make and last for many years if kept away from direct sun and moisture.

If possible, it's best to use partially dried herbs. They're still pliable enough to handle without crumbling and yet stiff enough not to wilt after the wreath is completed. In addition, most of the shrinkage due to moisture loss is past, so the finished wreath will remain full. If fresh greens are used, mildew can result if they're too solidly packed together; if too loosely arranged, the wreath may look bare.

Different wreath bases can be used, depending on the look you desire. A ring of stiff, rippled wire produces a narrow, flat wreath. A flat plastic foam circle will produce a fuller wreath of medium width. For a very full, rounded wreath use a base of plastic foam molded over a wire ring (florists use these for funeral wreaths). Other shapes and sizes other than those available from a florist, craft, or garden shop can be made at home from plywood or a wire coat hanger.

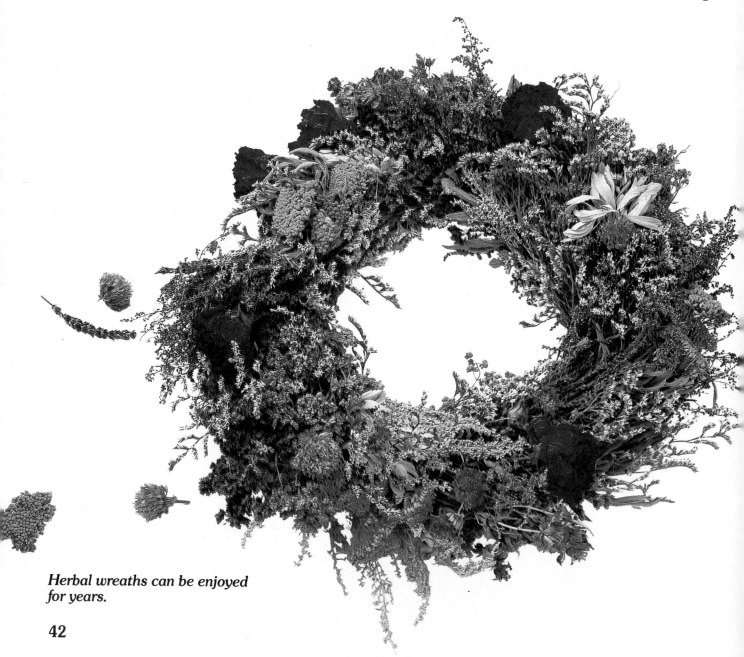

Herbal wreaths can be enjoyed for years.

Grape vines, heavy rope, woven rattan, and straw rings can all be used to create unique designs.

Stiff-stemmed herbs can be wrapped with florist wire or, in the case of plastic foam, pushed into the base. Those with weak or small stems should be gathered into small bundles and wired to a wooden stem or florist's pick (available at floral supply and many craft stores). They can then be handled the same as those with stiff stems.

Completed herbal wreaths are as varied as the greens that are used to make them. Use a single species or a mixture of herbs. Different combinations will look delicate and airy, dense and handsome, or just plain homey. They combine nicely with other dried materials such as baby's breath and statice, too. Be creative.

Herbal Wreath

1. Use hand pruners to cut partially dried herb branches into 5-inch pieces.

2. Use a spool of florist wire or twine to attach the plant materials to the wire base. Lay a bundle of two or three pieces of herb on top of the heavy wire base, then wrap the twine firmly for three or four turns around both the base and the herb stems starting halfway down the stems and spiralling down toward the cut ends. Lay another bundle on top of the first one's stems, allowing the attractive section to show, and continue spiral wrapping. Lay each additional bundle on top of the preceding one until you've gone all the way around the form. Fill in until the entire base is covered and the wreath is as full as you desire.

3. Gently lift the first bundle of the circle in order to squeeze the last one or two bundles in. Flatten the lifted bundle back over the final ones by gently massaging it in place with your hand. Hang the wreath and adjust where needed: add pieces to thin or narrow spots and thin or trim with pruning shears where the greenery is too dense or straggling.

4. Leave the wreath lying flat until the herbs are completely dried out before hanging it up. This will avoid the possibility of the wreath becoming misshapen due to further drying. If desired, decorate the wreath further. Wreaths are also attractive when laid flat on a table. For example, you may use a wreath to surround a punch bowl or a candlestick base.

HERBS FOR DRIED ARRANGEMENTS

FOLIAGE:	Southernwood	Lavender-Cotton
Chervil	Thyme	Marjoram
Chives	Wormwood	Oregano
Horehound		Tansy
Lavender	FLOWERS:	
Lavender-Cotton	Chives	SEED HEADS:
Rosemary	Garlic Chives	Dill
Sage	Lavender	Rue

POTPOURRIS AND SACHETS

Potpourris are a mixture of sweet-scented petals, leaves, and spices that slowly release their perfume as an air freshener. They can be stored in a decorative airtight container that is opened for brief periods as needed. When left open continuously, the aromatic properties are quickly lost, but do perfume the room. Sachets are small packets of concentrated scent that can be slipped into bureau drawers or clothes and linen closets where they add a subtle fragrance to stored belongings.

Potpourris are quickly made, since the herbs, petals, and spices are simply stirred together and stored. A potpourri that is losing strength can often be revitalized by simply dropping two or three drops of essential oil into the container and covering it tightly for a few days. Sachets take a bit more work, as the ingredients are ground, then usually sewn or wrapped in fabric. Sachet bags can be made from netting, silks, satins, and laces for a feeling of opulent luxury. They can also be made from plain cottons or ginghams to echo a simple country theme.

All you need to make potpourri are petals, leaves, and spices.

Potpourri

1. Assemble dried herbs, citrus peels, spices, orris root powder, and essential oils. Combine the scents you find pleasing, using larger amounts of those with more delicate scents and smaller quantities of those that are strongly scented. Add essential oils one drop at a time. Mix gently and thoroughly. Be very cautious as these oils can easily overpower any other ingredients.

2. When the blend suits you, mix in 1 tablespoon chopped orris root to each cup of mixture. This fixes the scent to make it last longer. Store for 6 to 8 weeks in an airtight container in a dark, dry place to allow the fragrances to blend.

3. Spoon the mixture loosely into a nice-looking container with a tight-fitting top. Set it in a convenient location where it can be opened to release its perfume whenever you like.

To make a sachet, just use a mortar and pestle to pound potpourri into a medium to fine powder. Spoon it into a bag made of tightly woven fabric and sew the bag securely shut.

POTPOURRI AND SACHET MAKING

Angelica	Costmary	Marjoram
Basil	Geraniums, Scented	Rosemary
Chamomile	Hyssop	Sweet Woodruff
Chervil	Lavender	Thyme
Coriander	Lavender-Cotton	Wormwood

HERBAL ARRANGEMENTS

Herbs make especially attractive additions to fresh or dried floral arrangements. Many have foliage of unusual texture, color, or both, adding visual interest and variety to an arrangement. Good examples are rugged angelica, gray-green needled lavender, silvery knobbed lavender-cotton, purple basil, and densely ruffled parsley. They are also fragrant, giving an arrangement an added bonus. Since herbs are usually very long-lasting, they'll look great in a fresh flower arrangement for as long or longer than flowers.

Most herbs are not well known for their flowers, but a few do have nice blooms for fresh use. These include nasturtium, borage, calendula, chamomile, oregano, tansy, lavender, and chives. The latter four also dry well for use in winter bouquets.

Also appealing are the flat umbel flowers of dill, caraway, and coriander. These make airy star-like additions to arrangements while in bloom as well as later when their seedpods develop.

Lovely European herb basket.

**HERBS
FOR FRESH
ARRANGEMENTS**

FOLIAGE:
Angelica
Basil
Garlic Chives
Horehound
Lavender
Lavender-Cotton
Rue
Southernwood
Wormwood

FLOWERS:
Borage
Calendula
Chives
Garlic Chives
Lavender
Lavender-Cotton
Nasturtium
Oregano
Tansy

SEED HEADS:
Caraway
Dill
Rue

European Herb Basket

1. In a large basket that is lined with plastic, place pots of assorted herbs.

2. Add a container filled with floral foam in the basket so that cut flowers can be added. Add the cut flowers to the floral foam.

3. Cover the pots with moss.

Preserving With Glycerine

Since herbs used in arrangements will not be eaten, an alternative way to preserve them is with glycerine. Mix together 1 part glycerine (available at most drugstores) and 2 parts hot water in a jar and stir well. Cut the fresh herb stems at an angle with a sharp knife or scissors and arrange them in the jar in 3 or more inches of liquid. Leave them in this solution, topping up the mixture as the level goes down. You'll notice a color change as the glycerine slowly rises up into the leaves. After two weeks to a month when fully changed in color, remove the herbs from the solution. Materials preserved this way stay pliable and remain useful for several years. Store them in a dry place so that the glycerine will not attract water.

Tussy Mussies

1. Tussy mussies are a lovely, old-fashioned way to display and give away fresh herbs. Using an oasis holder (which can be purchased at craft stores), place a flower—a rosebud or a tansy cluster—in the center by inserting the stem into the oasis. Add additional small pieces of each kind of herb desired around the center, rotating as you work, until the nosegay is 2 to 4 inches across.

2. If you do not want to use an oasis holder, you may use a flower for the center and then add herbs around it. Wrap the stems together in floral tape, then place the bouquet inside a decorative paper doily, a ring of wilt-resistant leaves such as ivy, or a lace circle. Add a small ribbon bow, if you want more color.

Cosmetic Uses

Unless you have a very large garden to provide a generous supply of the necessary herbs, as well as the equipment for distilling herbal oils, the most sensible approach is to buy the ingredients from which to concoct your own products. Your local health supply store will probably stock most of what you need: scented waters, essential oils, dried herbs and flowers, powdered orris, and other herbal powders. Isopropyl rubbing alcohol, unscented talc, and a few herbal oils are available in many drugstores.

Baths The simplest method for preparing an herbal bath is to gather together several sprigs of one or more fresh or dried herb favorites and hold them under the tap while very hot water flows over them to fill the tub. To avoid having bits of leaves and flowers in the water, place the sprigs inside a fine-meshed drawstring bag and hang it under the tap or let it float in the water while the tub is filling. Squeeze the bag in the bathwater, setting it aside once the tub is filled. Discard the herbs and let the bag dry completely before using it again.

Another approach is to add just one or two drops of essential oil to the tap water as the tub is filling. Remember that these oils are highly concentrated.

Finally, herbs can be added to the tub in the form of bath salts. Mix together 2 parts regular baking soda, 1 part powdered orris root, and 2 to 3 drops of an herbal oil such as lavender or rosemary for every 3 ounces of soda/orris mixture. Mix well and store in an airtight container.

Dusting Powders Body powders are easily made by adding very finely powdered herbs that have been sifted or a few drops of essential oils to a scentless talcum powder or a homemade powder made from 5 ounces powdered orris, 9 ounces cornstarch, and 2 ounces rice flour. When using essential oils, add 8 drops of oil, one drop at a time, to each pound of powder. Mix very thoroughly with a mortar and pestle to distribute the oil evenly throughout the powder base. Some people are allergic to orris root. In this case, the powder can be made without it.

Cleansing Facial Steam To create a pore-cleansing facial steam, simply add about 1 tablespoon of fresh or 1½ tablespoons of dry herbs to a quart of boiling water in a prewarmed bowl. Keeping your eyes closed, hang your face over the bowl and cover both your head and the bowl with a bath towel tent. Allow the vapor to rise around your face for about 5 to 10 minutes; if it becomes too uncomfortable, take a break by removing the tent for a minute, then continue the treatment. At the end of treatment, splash your face with lukewarm water, then with cold water. You may also use cotton balls to apply an astringent lotion if your skin is especially oily. These final steps are necessary to close the pores the steam opened.

Astringent Facial Scrub For those with oily skin, a cleansing facial scrub can be made by mixing dry oatmeal or cornstarch (as a thickener) to lemon juice or cider vinegar, mixed with dried sage, yarrow, or chamomile.

Rinses To give a nice shine to your hair after washing it, you need to plan ahead. Prepare the rinse in advance, using a tablespoon of dried herbs to a quart of boiling water. Allow the mixture to steep for a half hour, then strain out the herbs. Pour this infusion over your hair as a final rinse after shampooing. Calendula petals, chamomile, and rosemary are nice choices.

Perfumed Toilet Waters Although the manufacture of perfumes is best left to commercial producers, it's possible to successfully produce a pleasant perfumed toilet water at home. Simply add a few drops of essential oil—lavender, rose, orange, and lemon are most often used—to a quart of isopropyl alcohol and shake well every day for one week. Then pour into small, tightly closed bottles to retain the delicate fragrance.

Herbal cosmetics have been popular for centuries.

Herb Encyclopedia

In the following pages, 41 of the most common and popular herbs are described. Each profile includes a photograph and a written description of the plant's habit of growth; details of site preferences; propagation; the best harvest time; and methods of preservation and storage. There are also notes on the following uses for each species: culinary, cosmetic, potpourri and sachet, and fresh or dried arrangement material. Since most herbs aren't noted for their blooms and many have inconspicuous or unimportant flowers, floral color is only noted for those few that have decorative blossoms.

The figures given for height and spread are the size normally reached by each species when mature. Keep in mind that these are only approximate: Ultimate size depends heavily on climate, soil, and light conditions. There can also be varietal differences involved. Therefore, regard these dimensions more as a guide than as a precise measure. You can depend on the fact that tall herbs will be consistently tall; low and spreading plants will reliably follow their particular growth habit.

Use this section to learn more details about the particular herbs that interest you. Use it also to find the information you want when making a garden plan. The brief, to-the-point format will help you to quickly make the best choices for your needs.

Many herbs grow very well indoors as potted plants.

Angelica

Anise

Basil

Biennial
Botanical Name: *Angelica archangelica*
Height: 60 to 72 inches
Spread: 36 inches
Description: This large, boldly attractive biennial has very lush growth, making it a striking focal point in the garden. It is similar in appearance to celery and parsnip plants. The flowers are white umbels followed by decorative yellow-green seedpods. Its flavor is licoricelike.
Ease of Care: Easy
How to Grow: Angelica likes a cool, moist location and average to well-drained soil. It will grow in sun or partial shade. Sow seeds in place or transplant them when still very small as they don't like to be moved. One plant is enough to supply the needs of an average family.
Propagation: By seed. Seeds must be no more than a few weeks old to be viable. Sow in late fall or early spring while the ground is still cool. Leave seeds on top of the soil; do not cover them.
Uses: Fresh leaves—soups, stews
    Dried leaves—salads, soups, stews, potpourris
    Fresh foliage—floral arrangements
    Seeds—teas, baked goods
    Stems—candy, pork, baked goods
    Dried roots—teas, breads
    Root oil—baths, lotions
Preservation: Harvest stems during second spring, leaves throughout summer season, roots in fall, and seeds when ripe. Stems can be candied or frozen. Hang-dry or freeze leaves, depending on planned use.

Annual
Botanical Name: *Pimpinella anisum*
Height: 18 to 24 inches
Spread: 4 to 8 inches
Description: Feathery leaves and a lacy flower umbel are held on a tall and not very strong stem. These annuals look similar to dill and, like that plant, do best when grown closely together either in rows or clumps so that the multiple stems provide support for one another. The flavor is licoricelike.
Ease of Care: Easy, but it will take at least 4 frost-free months to grow seeds to maturity. Therefore, in northern areas only the leaves can be obtained from home-grown plants.
How to Grow: Plant in full sun and average, light dry soil. Either seed in place where they'll grow or transplant them when they are very small.
Propagation: By seed in early spring.
Uses: Fresh or frozen leaves—salads, cottage cheese, teas, jellies
    Seeds—perfumes, soaps, breads, cookies, fish stocks, teas, soups, stews
Preservation: Harvest leaves during late summer for freezing. Harvest seeds when fully ripe, watching carefully to cut plants at ground level when first seeds ripen. Hang-dry the seed heads inside paper bags in a warm, dry place. Store them in tightly sealed containers.

Annual
Botanical Name: *Ocimum basilicum*
Height: 18 inches
Spread: 10 inches
Description: Basil has a very neat, dense growing habit with attractive, glossy, bright-green, triangular leaves. All varieties of this good-looking annual make effective additions to any garden. They can also be clipped into a neat hedging, if desired. Flowers are not an important feature.
Ease of Care: Easy
How to Grow: Full sun and rich, moist soil are preferred. Sow seeds when soil is warm, or get a head start by starting them indoors and transplanting seedlings to the garden after danger of frost is past.
Propagation: By seed outdoors in late spring or indoors 8 weeks before the last frost.
Uses: Fresh, dried, and frozen leaves—vinegars, sauces, stews, salads, fish, shellfish, chicken, veal, lamb, tomatoes, potatoes
    Dried leaves—potpourris, sachets
    Fresh branches—floral arrangements
    Cosmetic uses—hair rinses, toilet waters, soaps
Preservation: The ideal harvest time, when flavor is at its peak, is when flower buds are about to blossom. Prunings can be used whenever they are taken. Hang-dry and store in airtight containers; better flavor is retained if frozen or stored in oil or vinegar.
Other Varieties: Compact dwarf variety, "Spicy Globe," makes an outstanding edging or an attractive container plant. "Purple Ruffles" and "Dark Opal" are two dramatic, purple-leaved varieties. "Green Ruffles" has a great lime-green color. Lemon basil has a distinct lemon flavor.

Borage

Burnet

Calendula, Pot Marigold

Annual to Biennial
Botanical Name: *Borago officinalis*
Height: 24 to 30 inches
Spread: 18 inches
Description: A basal rosette of long, spear-shaped leaves produces tall stems covered with attractive, bright-blue, star-shaped flowers that hang downward. Borage is a nice addition to any flower garden. All parts of the plant are densely covered with hairs. The flavor is similar to cucumber. Although usually grown as an annual, this plant will often overwinter in mild climates for a second growing season.
Ease of Care: Easy
How to Grow: Borage prefers a dry, sunny location in poor to ordinary, well-drained soil. It is difficult to transplant; move when very young if it must be moved at all.
Propagation: By seed in early spring or late fall.
Uses: Fresh leaves—fruit drinks
　　　　Flowers—salads, pickles, candy, cheeses, fish, poultry, vegetables, floral arrangements
Preservation: Pick blossoms as they open and use them fresh or candy them. Leaves are good for fresh use at any time. Since much of the flavor is lost during drying, preserve as a flavored vinegar for winter use.

Perennial
Botanical Name: *Poterium sanguisorba*
Height: 18 inches
Spread: 12 inches
Description: A low, ground-hugging rosette of dark green leaves forms the basic plant from which 12- to 18-inch thin flower stems arise. This perennial is frequently grown as an annual in order to obtain the best flavor and most tender leaves. The flavor is that of cucumber.
Ease of Care: Easy
How to Grow: Grow in full sun in average soil, although rich soil improves its flavor. Burnet prefers an alkaline soil; where soil is very acid, lime should be added. Young seedlings can be moved.
Propagation: By seed; burnet will self-sow easily after first planting.
Uses: Fresh leaves—salads, wine punches, cheese spreads
Preservation: Harvest leaves in early autumn and store them as flavored vinegar.

Annual
Botanical Name: *Calendula officinalis*
Height: 12 to 24 inches
Spread: 12 inches
Description: Very coarse, bright-green, strap-shaped leaves are held rather stiffly on the stems. Growth is brittle and snaps off fairly easily. This annual grows rapidly and blooms abundantly all summer until after the first frost. Flower colors range from bright yellow to vivid orange. Calendula is a cheerful addition to any flower bed and is very attractive as a pot plant indoors or out.
Ease of Care: Easy
How to Grow: Calendulas enjoy full sun and average, well-drained soil. Sow them directly in the garden or start them early indoors for transplanting to the garden after the last frost. Insects like calendulas, so be careful to eradicate them if they appear.
Propagation: By seed outdoors in the early spring or indoors 6 to 7 weeks before the last frost.
Uses: Fresh petals—salads, soups, wine punches, cheeses, poultry
　　　　Dried petals—hair rinses, baths
　　　　Fresh flowers (complete)—floral arrangements
Preservation: Remove petals from blossoms and spread them thinly on screening to dry. Grind them to a powder and store in an airtight container.

Caraway

Catnip, Catmint

Chamomile

Biennial
Botanical Name: *Carum carvi*
Height: 24 inches
Spread: 8 inches
Description: These biennials have finely cut leaves that strongly resemble carrot foliage. The white umbel flowers develop in the second year to produce the distinctively flavored seeds.
Ease of Care: Average
How to Grow: Caraway grows best in a light, dry, well-drained soil in full sun, although it will tolerate partial shade. Mulching will provide the moist growing conditions caraway prefers. Plant in place as caraway has a taproot and does not transplant easily.
Propagation: By seed outdoors in early spring or late summer.
Uses: Fresh leaves—salads, soups, stews
Seeds—breads, sauerkraut, beef, pork, cheeses, potatoes, fish. Add during the last few minutes of cooking.
Fresh root—use as a winter vegetable like parsnip in soups and stews
Preservation: Harvest seeds when fully ripe, watching carefully to cut plants at ground level when first seeds ripen. Hang-dry the seed heads inside paper bags in a cool, dry place. Store in tightly sealed containers. In its first fall or spring, dig up roots, clean them, and store them in a root cellar or a similar root crop storage area.

Perennial
Botanical Name: *Nepeta cataria*
Height: 18 to 24 inches
Spread: 15 inches
Description: Fuzzy, gray-green, triangular leaves grow in pairs along branches. An abundance of branches forms a dense perennial mat that gives off a pungent scent when crushed. Cats enjoy lying and rolling on catnip because of its aroma.
Ease of Care: Easy
How to Grow: Catnip grows well in full sun to partial shade in average to sandy, well-drained soil.
Propagation: By seed in spring or fall; by cuttings of active growth in early summer.
Uses: Fresh leaves—candied
Dried leaves—teas, cat toys
Preservation: Gather them in late summer just before they are in full bloom. Hang-dry the plants, remove leaves from stems, and store them in airtight containers.

Perennial
Botanical Name: *Chamaemelum nobile*
Height: 9 to 12 inches
Spread: 4 to 6 inches
Description: These fine-leaved, small plants look almost like ferns, but they have a very strong aromatic scent. Over time, perennial chamomile will spread by means of underground shoots to form a solid mat that, if desired, can be kept mowed about 3 inches high. It produces an abundance of small, daisy-type flowers.
Ease of Care: Easy
How to Grow: Chamomile grows in full sun in average to poor soils that are light and dry. Plant them in a group; a single plant is too small to have any impact.
Propagation: By seed in early spring; by division in spring or fall.
Uses: Dried flowers—teas, lotions
Dried plants—hair rinses, baths, potpourris
Preservation: Harvest whole plants or flowers when petals begin to turn back onto the center. Hang-dry plants; screen dry flowers.
Other Varieties: German chamomile (*Matricaria recutita*) is very similar and is used in the same ways as the perennial chamomile. However, since it's an annual, it must be grown from seed each spring. It grows to 24 inches and cannot be mowed.

Chervil

Chives

Coriander, Cilantro

Annual
Botanical Name: *Anthriscus cerefolium*
Height: 18 inches
Spread: 4 to 8 inches
Description: Lacy, fernlike, dark green leaves have a coarser texture than carrot foliage, but finer than parsley. Chervil has a very delicate flavor of a licorice/parsley blend. Of the two forms available, the curly variety is more decorative in the garden than the flat variety.
Ease of Care: Average to difficult.
How to Grow: Chervil likes coolness and does well in partial shade. It likes a moist, well-drained, average or better soil. Do not try to move plants. For a fresh supply throughout the season, plant at 3-week intervals.
Propagation: By seed in the fall or very early spring.
Uses: Fresh or frozen leaves—eggs, salads, soups, fish, stews, veal. Add during the last few minutes of cooking.
  Dried flowers—floral arrangements
  Dried leaves—potpourris
Preservation: Pick chervil just before blooming. For culinary use, freeze leaves or store them in a small amount of oil. For potpourri, dry rapidly in an oven and store immediately.

Perennial
Botanical Name: *Allium schoenoprasum*
Height: 8 to 12 inches
Spread: 8 inches
Description: Chives have very tight clumps of long, skinny, grasslike onion leaves. They produce an abundance of small, rosy purple, globe-shaped flowers in early summer. They can be used as edging plants, grown alone, or with other plants in containers. Chives have a mild onion flavor.
Ease of Care: Easy
How to Grow: This herb prefers an average to rich, moist soil, but will manage in almost any soil if kept moist. It grows in full sun to partial shade. It can also be grown as a pot plant indoors any time of the year for a source of fresh supply.
Propagation: By seed or division taken at any time during the growing season.
Uses: Fresh, dried, or frozen leaves—cream cheese spreads, cottage cheese, potatoes, salads, eggs, soups, poultry, fish, shellfish, veal. Add during the last few minutes of cooking.
  Fresh flowers—vinegars, salads, garnishes
  Dried flowers—floral arrangements, wreaths
Preservation: Harvest only part of the plant at a time for continuous production through the season. Mince leaves and then freeze them for full flavor; dried leaves are less flavor-filled. Hang-dry the flowers for decorative uses. Pick them before any seeds begin to appear.

Annual
Botanical Name: *Coriandrum sativum*
Height: 24 to 36 inches
Spread: 6 inches
Description: The bright green, lacy leaves look very similar to flat-leaved Italian parsley on the lower part of this plant, also known as Chinese Parsley, but become more finely fernlike further up. This large annual has a leaf and root flavor that is a cross between sage and citrus; the seeds, however, are simply citruslike.
Ease of Care: Easy
How to Grow: Plant in rich, well-drained soil in sun. Coriander plants are best located where they are protected from the wind, since they blow over easily.
Propagation: By seed once the soil is warm in spring.
Uses: Fresh or frozen leaves—potatoes, clams, oysters
  Seeds—marinades, cheeses, pickles, mushrooms, stews, curries, chicken, quick breads, potpourri
  Fresh roots—salads, relishes
Preservation: Harvest only fresh, young leaves and freeze them promptly. Harvest seeds when they have turned brown, but are not yet released. Cut a whole plant and hang-dry inside paper bags to catch seeds.

Costmary

Perennial
Botanical Name: *Chrysanthemum balsamita*
Height: 30 to 36 inches
Spread: 24 inches
Description: Basal clusters of elongated oval leaves look similar to horseradish growth. This perennial sends up tall flower stems that produce clusters of unremarkable blooms. When the leaves are young and fresh, they're mint scented; the scent changes to balsam when the leaves are dried.
Ease of Care: Easy
How to Grow: Grow in fertile, well-drained soil, in full sun to partial shade. Divide every few years as the clump becomes too large.
Propagation: By division as needed.
Uses: Fresh leaves—tuna fish, shrimp, eggs, lemonade
Dried leaves—sachets, potpourris, baths, lotions
Preservation: Pick leaves when they are young and tender for immediate fresh use or a few at a time to dry. Costmary retains its scent for a long period when dried.

Dill

Annual
Botanical Name: *Anethum graveolens*
Height: 24 to 36 inches
Spread: 6 inches
Description: Dill has extremely fine cut, fernlike leaves on tall stems. It is a blue-green annual with attractive yellow flower umbels and yellow-green seed heads.
Ease of Care: Easy
How to Grow: Dill likes acid, light, moist, and sandy soil in full sun. Since it does not transplant well, sow it in place and thin. Grow it in clumps or rows so stems can give support to one another.
Propagation: By seed in late fall or early spring. Plant at 3-week intervals during spring and early summer for a fresh supply all season.
Uses: Fresh leaves—potatoes, tomatoes, vinegars, pickles, fish, shrimp, stews, cheeses, lamb, pork, poultry
Fresh and dried seed heads—floral arrangements
Seeds—pickles, cheeses
Preservation: Clip fresh leaves as needed. Flavor is best retained for winter use if frozen; pick the leaves just as flowers begin to open. For seeds, harvest entire plants when seed heads are brown but not yet releasing seeds. Hang-dry in paper bags to catch seeds.

Fennel

Perennial
Botanical Name: *Foeniculum vulgare*
Height: 50 to 72 inches
Spread: 18 to 36 inches
Description: Fennel has very fine cut leaves that look very similar to dill. This half-hardy perennial has a sweetish, licoricelike flavor. The flowers and seed heads are attractive and make appealing additions to floral arrangements.
Ease of Care: Easy
How to Grow: Fennel likes alkaline soil; add lime if soil is very acid. Grow in full sun in well-drained, rich soil. Locate them where plants are sheltered from heavy winds since they blow over easily.
Propagation: By seed in cold climates, where it will grow as an annual. Sow in late fall or early spring.
Uses: Fresh leaves—sauces, salads, eggs, fish. Add during the last few moments of cooking.
Dried leaves—cosmetic oils, soaps, facials
Seeds—desserts, cakes, breads, potatoes, spreads
Preservation: Snip individual leaves to use fresh or to freeze. Harvest whole plants just before blooming and hang-dry. To harvest seeds, cut down entire plants when seeds turn brown but before they release. Hang-dry in paper bags to catch the seeds.
Other Varieties: Sweet fennel, *Foeniculum vulgare dulce*, is a closely related annual, the base stems of which are eaten as a vegetable in the same manner as celery.

Garlic Chives

Geraniums, Scented

Horehound

Perennial
Botanical Name: *Allium tuberosum*
Height: 18 inches
Spread: 8 inches
Description: Garlic chives (also known as Chinese Chives and Chinese Leeks) have compact, grasslike clumps of large, flattened, blue-green leaves that look like a larger version of chives. This perennial has attractive, white, globe-shaped blossoms that last a long time in floral arrangements. It has a definite garlic flavor.
Ease of Care: Easy
How to Grow: Plant seeds in full sun in average to poor soil.
Propagation: By seed in spring; by division anytime during the growing season.
Uses: Fresh leaves—salads, soups, spreads, vinegars
Dried leaves—soups, cheeses, sauces
Fresh and dried flowers—floral arrangements
Preservation: Harvest only part of the plant at a time for continuous production throughout the season. Mince leaves and then freeze them for full flavor; drying causes some flavor loss. Hang-dry flowers for decorative uses.

Half-Hardy Perennial
Botanical Name: *Pelargonium* species
Height: Varies with variety
Spread: Varies with variety
Description: These aromatic-leaved perennials come in a variety of scents, including rose, orange, pepper, lemon, lime, mint, and apple. The leaf shapes are also varied, ranging from round to deeply cut, and their color ranges from yellow-green to reddish-purple according to the variety involved. Most make attractive potted plants and several have nice-looking flowers.
Ease of Care: Average
How to Grow: All prefer full sun and well-drained, rich to average soil. Geraniums overwinter as pot plants in cold climates.
Propagation: By cuttings before flowering.
Uses: Fresh leaves—cakes, cookies, jellies
Dried leaves—potpourris, sachets, baths, facials, teas
Fresh flowers—salads
Preservation: Pick single leaves just as plants begin to develop flower buds and dry them on screens.
Varieties: Lemon geranium is *P. mellissinum,* lime is *P. nervosum,* apple is *P. odoratissimum,* and peppermint is *P. tomentosum.* These are probably the most common of the many special scented geranium varieties available; choose those you prefer from the selection offered by your local plant supplier.

Perennial
Botanical Name: *Marrubium vulgare*
Height: 30 inches
Spread: 12 inches
Description: Horehound has attractive, round, gray, mintlike foliage. The overall look of this perennial is that of a woolly gray bush. It makes an attractive addition to any garden. Flower arrangers will find it an outstanding decorative foliage for fresh or dried use.
Ease of Care: Easy
How to Grow: Grow in full sun in average to poor, well-drained soil.
Propagation: By seed or division in late spring.
Uses: Fresh or dried leaves—candy flavorings, teas
Dried branches—floral arrangements
Preservation: Remove the leaves from the stems at the time of flowering and dry them on screens. Store in airtight containers. Hang-dry whole branches.

Horseradish

Perennial
Botanical Name: *Armoracia rusticana*
Height: 36 to 60 inches
Spread: 18 to 24 inches
Description: Horseradish is a perennial with a deep, spreading root topped with a cluster of large, coarse, yellow-green leaves. The root has a very sharp, radishlike flavor.
Ease of Care: Easy
How to Grow: Plant in full sun to partial shade, in well-drained soil.
Propagation: By seed or division in the spring; by root cuttings in early summer.
Uses: Fresh leaves—baths
  Roots—ground with white vinegar or mayonnaise to accompany fish, beef, potato salads, beets
Preservation: Harvest roots in late fall and store in root cellar or similar winter storage area for root crops. When ready to use, peel, grind, put into a glass jar, and mix and cover with white vinegar; store in refrigerator.

Hyssop

Perennial
Botanical Name: *Hyssopus officinalis*
Height: 18 inches
Spread: 12 inches
Description: This neat, low, shrubby plant has leaves growing in whorls around stiff, upright stems. It makes a good edging plant and can be clipped in order to keep its shape. This attractive perennial has a mintlike, but bitter flavor.
Ease of Care: Average
How to Grow: Prefers full sun, but can tolerate partial shade. Plant it in well-drained soil that is high in lime. Cut hyssop back each spring to encourage new growth.
Propagation: By division in the spring; by seed in late summer for early spring; by cuttings taken in early summer or by layering.
Uses: Fresh leaves—salads, soups, fruit salads, lamb, poultry, teas
  Dried leaves—teas, perfumes, potpourris, baths, facials
Preservation: Harvest hyssop just as it's about to flower. Hang-dry and use it whole for facials and baths, or remove leaves from stems for use in tea or potpourri.

Lavender

Perennial
Botanical Name: *Lavandula angustifolia*
Height: 36 to 48 inches
Spread: 18 to 30 inches
Description: Lavender has silver-gray, needlelike foliage on a bushy, spreading plant. This perennial grows about 2 to 3 feet high, then produces an abundance of 18- to 24-inch individual flower stalks topped by fragrant and attractive purple-blue, pink, or white clusters of bloom. It makes an outstanding year-round addition to any garden design. Lavender also makes a nice edging plant or pot plant. If desired, the smaller Munstead lavender can also be clipped to form a low hedge.
Ease of Care: Average
How to Grow: Grow in full sun in well-drained, sandy to poor soil.
Propagation: Lavender can easily be started from seed, propagated by cuttings before it flowers, or by layering. It prefers an alkaline soil.
Uses: Fresh leaves—vinegars, jellies
  Dried leaves—facials, baths
  Fresh flowers—candy, vinegars, floral arrangements
  Dried flowers—potpourris, sachets, perfumes, soaps, bath powders, wreaths, floral arrangements
  Dried branches—baths, wreaths, floral arrangements
Preservation: Pick separate leaves and 3- to 4-inch active growth tips in spring and summer. Dry on screens. Harvest flowers when they are in the late bud stage, just before they actually bloom. Hang-dry.
Other Varieties: There are a number of different species and cultivars of lavender available. The differences between them focus primarily on flower color, size, and growth habit. Choose the variety you like best for the uses you have in mind.

Lavender-Cotton

Lemon Balm

Lovage

Perennial
Botanical Name: *Santolina chamaecyparissus*
Height: 12 to 18 inches
Spread: 18 inches
Description: Evergreen, very light silver-gray, cottony foliage produces an interesting knobby look. The spreading plants are very dense-looking. They're great as edgings or clipped into low hedges. Each bright yellow, buttonlike flower grows on a separate stem.
Ease of Care: Easy
How to Grow: Lavender-Cotton or Santolina likes full sun and poor, sandy, preferably alkaline soil. It can be cut back each spring to encourage new growth. In very cold climates, you should either provide winter protection or grow plants in pots and bring them indoors for the cold season.
Propagation: By seed in spring, propagation by cuttings in early summer, or division by layering.
Uses: Dried leaves—potpourris, sachets
　　　Dried flowers—wreaths, floral
　　　　　arrangements
　　　Fresh branches—floral
　　　　　arrangements
　　　Dried branches—floral
　　　　　arrangements, baths
Preservation: Harvest foliage in late summer; flowers should be harvested just as they start to come into bloom. Hang-dry.

Perennial
Botanical Name: *Melissa officinalis*
Height: 48 inches
Spread: 18 inches
Description: A full, attractive perennial with shield-shaped leaves, lemon balm spreads readily by seed. As its name suggests, it smells of lemon.
Ease of Care: Easy
How to Grow: Lemon balm prospers in full sun, but will also do well in partial shade. It likes a well-drained or moist, sandy soil. It grows abundantly.
Propagation: By seed in the autumn or early spring; by cuttings in the spring and summer; by division in spring or fall.
Uses: Fresh leaves—salads, cold
　　　　　beverages, jellies
　　　　Dried leaves—potpourris, perfumes
Preservation: Pick in midsummer and hang-dry branches or spread single leaves on screening to dry.
Other Varieties: Bee balm, *Monarda didyma,* is not a related species, but is similar in its growth, propagation, and uses. It prefers moist, average to fertile soil for best growth.

Perennial
Botanical Name: *Levisticum officinalis*
Height: 60 inches
Spread: 30 inches
Description: Lovage is a large, handsome perennial plant with glossy, dark green, cut-leaf foliage that looks like dark-colored celery. The flavor is like that of celery, but somewhat sweeter and stronger. A single plant makes a dramatic garden focal point.
Ease of Care: Average
How to Grow: Lovage likes moist, rich, acid soil. It will grow in full sun or partial shade. Since it dies down completely during the winter, mark its place in the fall to avoid the possibility of digging into and damaging it.
Propagation: By seed in late summer; by division in autumn or early spring.
Uses: Fresh, frozen, or dried leaves—
　　　　　stews, soups
　　　Fresh leaves—salads
　　　Fresh stems—salads, soups,
　　　　　steamed vegetables
　　　Seeds—pickles, cheeses, salads,
　　　　　dressings, potatoes, tomatoes,
　　　　　chicken
Preservation: Use fresh as needed. Pick for winter use just before the plant begins to bloom. To freeze, blanch small amounts at a time, quick cool, and freeze as is, or chop and freeze in cubes. Alternatively, hang-dry. For seeds, pick seed heads when they turn brown but before they release. Hang-dry inside paper bags to catch seeds.

Marjoram

Perennial, often grown as Annual
Botanical Name: *Origanum majorana* or *Majorana hortensis*
Height: 8 to 12 inches
Spread: 12 to 18 inches
Description: Marjoram is a bushy, spreading, half-hardy perennial that is grown as an annual in climates where it freezes. It has small, oval, gray-green, velvety leaves. This plant is attractive when grown as a pot plant and brought indoors to overwinter.
Ease of Care: Easy
How to Grow: Marjoram likes rich, well-drained alkaline soil and full sun. Where winters are severe, treat it as an annual or as a pot plant. Locate it in a sheltered spot for best overwinter survival outdoors.
Propagation: By seed early indoors, transplanting seedlings outdoors after danger of frost has passed; by cuttings in spring.
Uses: Fresh or dried leaves—stuffings, soups, stews, meat loaf, pork, poultry, fish, eggs, potatoes, cheeses. Can be used in place of oregano.
Dried leaves—baths, potpourris, sachets
Dried flowers—floral arrangements, wreaths
Preservation: Snip fresh when needed. For drying, harvest just before flowering and hang-dry.

Nasturtium

Annual
Botanical Name: *Tropaeolum majus*
Height: 12 inches for bush, 72 inches for vines
Spread: 18 inches for bush
Description: Distinctive, blue-green circular leaves are held up on fleshy stems. These annuals come in a variety of types ranging from compact bushes to long-spreading vines. They make an eye-catching addition to any garden. In addition, they have large attractive blooms that range in color from palest yellows, pinks, and apricots to deep, rich yellows, oranges, and burgundy. The vining types are great in hanging planters, window boxes, or for use on trellises and fences. Aphids love nasturtiums, so be on the lookout for them.
Ease of Care: Easy
How to Grow: Plant in full sun to partial shade in average to poor, moist soil.
Propagation: By seed in late spring. They're large and can be planted individually where the plants are going to grow.
Uses: Fresh leaves and flowers—salads
Fresh flowers—floral arrangements
Unripe seeds and flower buds— pickled for salads
Preservation: Pickle unripe seeds in vinegar and use them in salads.

Oregano

Perennial
Botanical Name: *Origanum vulgare*
Height: 18 inches
Spread: 12 inches
Description: Oregano is a bushy, spreading perennial with abundant oval leaves and purple blooms. Be careful to get the correct species. To be sure of avoiding disappointment, buy a plant that you've tested by crushing a few leaves and smelling or tasting them beforehand. It should have the distinct aroma of oregano.
Ease of Care: Easy
How to Grow: Grow in full sun, in average to sandy and preferably alkaline soil (add lime generously if soil is acid).
Propagation: Buy your first plant, then by division, layering, or cuttings to obtain additional ones.
Uses: Fresh or dried leaves—tomatoes, cheeses, eggs, beef, pork, poultry, shellfish, potatoes, sauces
Flowers—floral arrangements
Dried branches—baths
Preservation: Clip fresh as needed. Harvest at the time of bloom and hang-dry or freeze.

Parsley

Peppermint

Rosemary

Biennial grown as Annual
Botanical Name: *Petroselinum crispum*
Height: 12 inches
Spread: 8 inches
Description: Attractive, rich, green, dense leaves form a rosette base. A biennial usually grown as an annual, parsley comes in two cut-leaf forms: ruffled and Italian. The latter has flat leaves and is stronger-flavored than the curly variety. The curly form makes a nice edging plant; both are also easily grown as indoor pot plants.
Ease of Care: Easy
How to Grow: Plant in place in full sun or partial shade in a moist, rich soil. Pre-soak seeds between several hours and overnight in warm water to help speed up germination.
Propagation: By seed once the soil is warm.
Uses: Fresh, dried, or frozen leaves—
    garnishes, potatoes, soups,
    sauces, pasta, poultry, jellies,
    baths, shampoos, lotions
Preservation: Snip as needed fresh. Hang-dry the flat variety; snip and freeze the curly variety.

Perennial
Botanical Name: *Mentha piperita*
Height: 24 to 30 inches
Spread: 12 inches
Description: Peppermint has dark green, spear-shaped leaves that come to a point. It has a neat, dense growth habit with tall stems arising from an underground network of spreading stems. Since it can become invasive, plant it in an isolated location or where it can be kept contained. Another alternative is to grow it as a pot plant.
Ease of Care: Easy
How to Grow: Likes full sun or partial shade and rich, moist soil.
Propagation: By cuttings taken in mid-summer; by division at any time during the growing season.
Uses: Fresh or frozen leaves—garnishes,
    vinegars, jellies, punches,
    candy, lamb
    Dried leaves—teas
Preservation: Pick shoots in early to mid-summer. Hang-dry or freeze.
Other Varieties: Pineapple mint, apple mint, and lemon mint each have flavors as indicated by their names. (Also refer to the profile on Spearmint.)

Perennial
Botanical Name: *Rosmarinus officinalis*
Height: 48 to 72 inches
Spread: 18 to 24 inches
Description: Rosemary is an attractive, evergreen perennial with a spreading habit of growth. Its gray-green, needle-shaped foliage can be pruned to form a low hedge. Grow rosemary as a pot plant in colder climates, protecting it from winter winds. It makes an attractive addition to any garden. There is a prostrate form that makes a wonderful ground cover where hardy.
Ease of Care: Average
How to Grow: Likes a sandy, alkaline soil and full sun.
Propagation: By cuttings or by seed in spring, or by layering.
Uses: Fresh or frozen leaves—fish, lamb,
    potatoes, soups, tomatoes,
    pork, poultry, cheeses, eggs,
    breads, fruit salads, jellies
    Dried leaves—facials, hair rinses,
    sachets, potpourris, lotions,
    toilet waters
    Fresh and dried branches—baths
Preservation: Pick rosemary fresh as desired. Hang-dry or freeze the active young 3- to 4-inch growth tips.

Rue

Perennial
Botanical Name: *Ruta graveolens*
Height: 24 inches
Spread: 18 inches
Description: This perennial has blue-green, teardrop-shaped foliage in clusters. Rue is an attractive and unusual plant to use as a focal point in a garden design.
Ease of Care: Average
How to Grow: Full sun in poor, sandy, alkaline soil. It can also be easily grown as a pot plant.
Propagation: By seed in spring or started ahead of time indoors and transplanted into the garden after the danger of frost has passed; by cuttings in mid-summer.
Uses: Fresh leaves—floral arrangements, tussy mussies
Dried seed heads—floral arrangements
Preservation: Pick just before flowers open and hang-dry. Collect seeds when flower heads ripen.
Other Varieties: The variety "Jackman's Blue" is compact and very blue leaved. It can also be trimmed to form a lovely low hedge.

Sage

Perennial
Botanical Name: *Salvia officinalis*
Height: 20 inches
Spread: 24 inches
Description: Sage is a perennial with gray-green, pebblelike, textured leaves in a long, oval shape. It has an attractive, compact, spreading growth habit. This plant is also available in variegated and purple-leaved varieties. Sage is a good edging plant and is attractive in any garden.
Ease of Care: Easy
How to Grow: Grow it in full sun in a well-drained sandy, alkaline soil. Protect it from the wind.
Propagation: By seed, cuttings, or division by layering in the spring.
Uses: Fresh, frozen, or dried leaves—salads, breads, soups, stews, pork, beef, fish, lamb, poultry, stuffings, tomatoes, vegetables, cheeses, teas
Dried branches—baths, lotions, herbal wreaths
Preservation: Use fresh sage as needed. Pick active growth shoots or separate leaves to hang-dry, screen dry, or freeze.
Other Varieties: Sage is available in gold and green variegated (*S. officinalis* 'Aurea') and purple-leaved (*S. officinalis* 'Purpurea') varieties.

Savory, Summer

Annual
Botanical Name: *Satureja hortensis*
Height: 18 inches
Spread: 8 inches
Description: This attractive annual has flattened, gray-green, needle-shaped leaves. The leaves are soft rather than stiff and have a slightly peppery flavor. The overall look of the plant is light and airy.
Ease of Care: Easy
How to Grow: Plant seeds in place in full sun in a light, rich to average soil. They do not transplant well. Summer savory grows well as a container plant with seeds planted directly in a pot.
Propagation: By seed when the soil is warm.
Uses: Fresh, dried, or frozen leaves—tomatoes, pastas, soups, stews, roasts, beans, salads, cheeses, fish, vinegars, vegetables
Preservation: When it begins to flower, dry it on screens or paper.

Sorrel, French

Southernwood

Spearmint

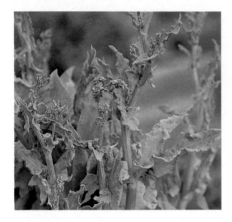

Perennial
Botanical Name: *Rumex acetosa* or *R. scutatus*
Height: 18 inches
Spread: 10 inches
Description: Succulent, bright green, spear-shaped leaves in a low rosette send up tall flower stalks that should be removed so that leaf supply will continue. The leaves of this hardy perennial have a pleasant acidity that brightens any salad. Sorrel can also be grown as an indoor pot plant.
Ease of Care: Easy
How to Grow: Provide full sun or partial shade in a moist, rich acid soil. Shady conditions produce a milder taste.
Propagation: By seed or division in spring.
Uses: Fresh or frozen leaves—soups, lamb, beef, sauces
Preservation: Remove single leaves and use them fresh or freeze them for winter use.

Perennial
Botanical Name: *Artemisia abrotanum*
Height: 30 inches
Spread: 24 inches
Description: Woolly, silver-gray, cut leaves and a dense, branching growth habit make these perennials a very decorative addition to any garden.
Ease of Care: Easy
How to Grow: Full sun in any kind of soil. Prune southernwood back each spring to encourage new growth and a nice shape.
Propagation: By semi-hardwood cuttings in late summer.
Uses: Fresh branches—floral arrangements, tussy mussies
Dried branches—baths, floral arrangements, wreaths
Preservation: Pick branches just before flowering and hang-dry.

Perennial
Botanical Name: *Mentha spicata* or *M. viridis*
Height: 20 inches
Spread: 12 inches
Description: Green, pointed leaves are somewhat hairy compared to peppermint, but the best way to tell them apart is to crush the leaves and taste or smell them. Spearmint has a neat, dense growth with tall stems arising from a network of spreading underground stems. It can become invasive, so plant it in an isolated location or where it can be kept contained. A good solution is to grow it as a pot plant.
Ease of Care: Easy
How to Grow: Full sun or partial shade in rich, moist soil.
Propagation: By cuttings in mid-summer; by division at any time during the growing season.
Uses: Fresh or frozen leaves—candy, garnishes, jellies, punches, lamb
Dried leaves—teas
Preservation: Pick shoots in early to mid-summer. Hang-dry or freeze.
Other Varieties: Pineapple mint, apple mint, and lemon mint each have distinctive flavors as indicated by their name. (Also refer to the profile on Peppermint.)

Sweet Woodruff

Tansy

Tarragon

Perennial
Botanical Name: *Galium odoratum* or *Asperula odorata*
Height: 6 to 8 inches
Spread: 6 to 8 inches
Description: Single, small, and knife-shaped leaves circle in tiers around the stem like flattened wheel spokes. This perennial has a rich green color and spreads by means of underground stems to make a lovely ground cover when it has its preferred growing conditions of shade and rich, moist soil.
Ease of Care: Difficult unless conditions are exactly to its liking.
How to Grow: Grow in rich, moist soil in fairly deep, woodland shade.
Propagation: By seed in fall that will sprout in the spring; by divisions after flowering.
Uses: Fresh leaves—wine punches
Dried leaves—potpourris, sachets, wreaths
Preservation: Pick fresh sweet woodruff as needed. Cut entire stems when they are in bloom and hang-dry.

Perennial
Botanical Name: *Tanacetum vulgare*
Height: 40 inches
Spread: 12 to 18 inches
Description: This hardy perennial has lush, dark green, cut leaves and tall flower stems that produce tight clusters of intense yellow, button-shaped blooms. These are vigorous growers that spread rapidly and can take over; keep them constantly under control or place them where they can be allowed to run wild. The foliage has a strong peppery odor and flavor.
Ease of Care: Easy
How to Grow: Grow in full sun or partial shade in average to poor soil.
Propagation: By seed in spring; by division in spring or fall; or by layering.
Uses: Fresh or dried flowers—floral arrangements
Preservation: Harvest leaves singly and dry them on screens or harvest entire stems with flowers and hang-dry.

Perennial
Botanical Name: *Artemisia dracunculus*
Height: 24 inches
Spread: 24 inches
Description: This bushy, medium green perennial has long, narrow, pointed leaves and inconspicuous flowers that rarely appear. Be sure to get the French rather than the Russian variety that looks very much the same with somewhat narrower and lighter green leaves. However, the latter has none of the sweetly aromatic flavor wanted for culinary use. Test it by crushing, smelling, and tasting a few leaves.
Ease of Care: Average
How to Grow: Likes full sun to partial shade in a sandy to rich alkaline soil that is well drained. It can also be grown success-fully as a pot plant. Cut it back in the fall or early spring. Protect it with a mulch during the winter in cold climates.
Propagation: Buy your first plant, then by cuttings in summer and fall; by division in early spring; or by layering.
Uses: Fresh, dried, or frozen leaves—fish, vinegars, tomatoes, salads, eggs, chicken, pickles. Add during the last few minutes of cooking.
Preservation: Pick separate leaves or 3- to 4-inch growth tips at any time for fresh use. Pick just before blooming to freeze or dry. Be careful because the delicate flavor is easily lost if dried too long. Store immediately in an airtight container. The flavor can also be captured in vinegar or oil.
Other Varieties: Since it does not produce seeds, if tarragon seeds are offered, they will be those of Russian rather than French tarragon. Buy plants only.

Thyme

Wormwood

Perennial
Botanical Name: *Thymus vulgaris*
Height: 1 to 10 inches depending on variety
Spread: 12 to 18 inches
Description: These tiny-leaved, wide-spreading perennials make a good and inexpensive ground cover. They can be clipped and mowed regularly, if desired. Their profuse blooms are especially attractive to bees; clip off flower heads just before blooming. The lowest-growing varieties are excellent to plant in flagstone walks.
Ease of Care: Easy
How to Grow: Thyme does well in full sun to partial shade in poor to average, well-drained soil. Trim it back each spring to encourage abundant new growth. It can also be grown as a pot plant.
Propagation: By seed or division in spring or fall; by cuttings in early summer; or by layering.
Uses: Fresh, frozen, or dried leaves—
            marinades, stuffings, soups,
            vinegars, poultry, shellfish, fish,
            cheeses
        Dried leaves—sachets, potpourris,
            floral arrangements, baths,
            facials, wreaths
        Dried flowers—sachets, lotions,
            baths
Preservation: Harvest anytime for fresh use. Pick before and during flowering to hang-dry.
Other Varieties: There are many different thyme species and varieties with self-descriptive names: woolly thyme, silver thyme, lemon thyme, and golden thyme. The variations in their foliage colors, growth habits, and flower colors make them all good candidates for use in garden designs.

Perennial
Botanical Name: *Artemisia absinthium*
Height: 30 to 48 inches
Spread: 15 to 20 inches
Description: A handsome, very fine cut-leaf, silver-green foliage and a spreading growth habit makes this an attractive perennial.
Ease of Care: Average
How to Grow: Plant in full sun in almost any kind of soil as long as it's alkaline. Add lime if soil is naturally acid.
Propagation: By seed or cuttings in summer; by division in spring or fall.
Uses: Fresh leaves—floral arrangements
            Dried leaves—sachets, floral
                arrangements, wreaths
Preservation: Harvest when in flower and hang-dry.